Faith as social capital

Faith as social capital

Connecting or dividing?

Robert Furbey, Adam Dinham, Richard Farnell, Doreen Finneron, Guy Wilkinson
with
Catherine Howarth, Dilwar Hussain, Sharon Palmer

JOSEPH ROWNTREE
FOUNDATION

First published in Great Britain in March 2006 by

The Policy Press
Fourth Floor, Beacon House
Queen's Road
Bristol BS8 1QU
UK

Tel no +44 (0)117 331 4054
Fax no +44 (0)117 331 4093
Email tpp-info@bristol.ac.uk
www.policypress.org.uk

© Sheffield Hallam University 2006

Published for the Joseph Rowntree Foundation by The Policy Press

ISBN-10 1 86134 837 1
ISBN-13 978 1 86134 837 1

British Library Cataloguing in Publication Data
A catalogue record for this book is available from the British Library.

Library of Congress Cataloging-in-Publication Data
A catalog record for this book has been requested.

The **Joseph Rowntree Foundation** has supported this project as part of its programme of research and innovative development projects, which it hopes will be of value to policy makers, practitioners and service users. The facts presented and views expressed in this report are, however, those of the authors and not necessarily those of the Foundation.

The statements and opinions contained within this publication are solely those of the authors and not of The University of Bristol or The Policy Press. The University of Bristol and The Policy Press disclaim responsibility for any injury to persons or property resulting from any material published in this publication.

The Policy Press works to counter discrimination on grounds of gender, race, disability, age and sexuality.

Cover design by Qube Design Associates, Bristol
Photograph of members of the 'Faith Together in Leeds 11' partnership supplied by kind permission of the Church Urban Fund. Photographer: Caroline Purday.
Printed in Great Britain by Hobbs the Printers Ltd, Southampton

Contents

Acknowledgements

The work of making connections is demanding enough without having to pause to talk to researchers. And so we express our warm thanks to the many people – so varied in faith, ethnicity, age and role – who shared with us their experiences of working across 'boundaries' in different contexts and in diverse ways. From the heavy weight of the interview transcripts and observation notes we have had to try to crystallise the key and recurring expressions of excitement, frustration and desire for change. We hope that we have been able to repay people's commitment by interpreting and communicating their experiences to a wider audience that includes those who have the power to act and support in various ways.

Our work has benefited greatly from the critical support and tenacity of the members of the Project Advisory Group:

Mr Raj Bali (Trustee of the Multi Faith Centre, Derby, and President of the Hindu Temple Geeta Bhavan, Derby)

Professor Irene Bruegel (South Bank University)

Dr Helen Cameron (Oxford Brookes University)

Dr Alison Gilchrist (Community Development Foundation)

Professor Gurharpal Singh (University of Birmingham)

Dr Maggie Keane (St Peter's Saltley Trust)

Mr Dilowar Khan (East London Mosque and the London Muslim Centre)

Mr David Rayner (Office of the Deputy Prime Minister)

Colleagues at our various workplaces have been generous in their encouragement and advice. We are particularly grateful to the management committee of the Faith-based Regeneration Network for enabling Doreen Finneron to give time to the project during 2005. We have also valued the work of Lisa Jones in managing our budget and Margaret Wood and Lin Owen in providing a fine transcription service.

The research has been made possible through the financial and practical support of the Joseph Rowntree Foundation and its staff.

In thanking everyone, we underline our own responsibility for the evidence and interpretations presented on the following pages.

Notes on the research group

Robert Furbey teaches Urban Sociology at Sheffield Hallam University and has researched and written on tenant participation, urban regeneration and the legacy and eclipse of council housing. With Catherine Howarth, Dilwar Hussain and Sharon Palmer, he is a member of the inter-denominational and inter Faith Commission on Urban Life and Faith initiated by the Bishops' Urban Panel of the Church of England.

Adam Dinham lectures and researches in Social Policy at Anglia Ruskin University. His interests include the politics of disadvantage, community development and regeneration, in particular as they relate to the engagement of faith communities. He read Theology and Religious Studies at Selwyn College, Cambridge before completing an MA in Applied Social Studies. He has practised as a social worker and community development worker and has a PhD in Politics and Community Development from Goldsmiths College, University of London.

Richard Farnell is Professor of Neighbourhood Renewal at Coventry University where he also contributes to the work of the Centre for Local Economic Development. He was a member of the Policy Action Team on Community Self-Help established by the Social Exclusion Unit. Richard is a trustee of the Church Urban Fund and also chairs the Keynote Housing Group.

Doreen Finneron is Executive Director of the Faith-Based Regeneration Network. Doreen worked in faith community regeneration in Manchester for 14 years. She was subsequently National Development Officer at the Church Urban Fund. Her publications include *Tools for regeneration: A holistic approach for faith communities* (with Rumman Ahmed and Harmander Singh) and *Building on faith: Faith buildings in neighbourhood renewal* (with Adam Dinham).

Guy Wilkinson is National Inter Faith Relations Adviser and Secretary for Inter Faith Relations to the Archbishop of Canterbury. Guy's working life has covered a wide variety of countries, cultures and employment sectors. He has served parishes in Coventry, Guildford and Birmingham dioceses and was Archdeacon of Bradford. He has a wide experience of living and working among people and communities of Faiths other than Christian, both in the UK and in Africa.

Catherine Howarth is a community organiser with London Citizens. She has worked in East London, running a campaign for a 'London Living Wage' among outsourced cleaning, security and catering staff. This brought together East London religious congregations and trade union branches into a permanent coalition working for social and economic justice. Previously, Catherine was senior researcher at the New Policy Institute, where her work included research on indicators of poverty and social exclusion in a project funded by the Joseph Rowntree Foundation.

Dilwar Hussain is Research Fellow at the Islamic Foundation, Leicester. He is on the editorial board of the journal *Encounters: Journal of Inter-Cultural Perspectives* and is involved in several UK and European research networks. He is a member of the Archbishop of Canterbury's Commission on Urban Life and Faith and is Fellow of the Royal Foundation of St Katherine's Contextual Theology Centre, London. He is also involved in various community organisations, including the Citizens Organising Foundation.

Sharon Palmer has worked in the field of strategy and policy development for both

governmental and non-governmental
organisations and networks in the fields of
economic development, social care, planning
and regional strategy and policy. Sharon was
also a member of Bishop's Council in the
Diocese of Birmingham. Here, she contributed
to the development and delivery of a
successful residential holiday programme for
young people within inner cities. She has also
worked with the Save the Children Fund in
Britain and overseas.

Introduction

There has been growing interest during the last 15 years – in the UK and elsewhere – in 'social capital' as a potential source of economic and social benefits. Over the same period both Conservative and Labour governments in the UK have looked to 'Faith communities' as 'partners' in a range of social policies and regeneration programmes. These two developments form the context for this study in which we explore the contribution of Faith[1] organisations and their members to social capital.

In choosing this research focus we are entering two arenas of controversy. The place of 'Faith' in public policy is strongly contested and in Chapter 2 we shall underline the capacity of religious belief and tradition to create retreat, division and conflict as well as engagement, connection and understanding. The London bombings of July 2005 provided a shocking further reminder of this as we were writing this report. The controversy over the concept of 'social capital', of course, is less visceral. Nevertheless, its validity is keenly debated. Again, we shall sketch some of the key misgivings in Chapter 2 as we develop the direction of our inquiry.

What position does this study adopt in relation to these disputes? First, we accept that the idea of 'social capital' embodies an important proposition – that people are enriched not only by their financial and physical assets or by the 'human capital' stemming from their skills and qualifications, but also by their social relationships and membership of social networks. Second, we have sought to develop

an inquiry that permits the identification of positive contributions by Faith organisations and individual believers to social capital while also locating limitations, barriers and the more negative consequences of Faith.

Government interest in 'social capital' and in 'Faith'

The interest of the UK government in both the idea of social capital and the role of Faith communities confirms the policy relevance of this research agenda. Social capital is seen as contributing to better educational attainment, lower crime levels, improved health, more active citizenship, better functioning labour markets and higher economic growth (PIU, 2002). This positive view has been bolstered by wider research that has identified social capital as a key consideration in the quest for sustainable neighbourhoods (see, for example, Green et al, 2005). Such potential is prompting careful study of all the sources, forms and expressions of social capital and how they might be harnessed. The government perceives a 'Faith sector' as one promising source.

Formal recognition of the significance of the potential of Faith communities and their organisations in public policy was first reflected in the Inner Cities Religious Council (ICRC), established in 1992. At the time of writing the ICRC is located within the Office of the Deputy Prime Minister (ODPM) as part of the Supporting Communities Programme in the Neighbourhood Renewal Unit. It functions as 'a forum for members of Faith communities to work with the Government on issues of regeneration, neighbourhood renewal, social inclusion, and other relevant cross-departmental policies and processes'. This forum is justified in the following terms:

---

1 When using 'Faith' as the equivalent of 'Religion', as for example in 'Faith community', we adopt the emerging practice of spelling the word with a capital. When combined with a prefix, such as 'inter' or 'multi', no hyphen is used. The prefix is lower case and 'Faith' upper case, as in 'inter Faith'.

The Christian, Hindu, Jewish, Muslim and Sikh communities in particular have a strong urban presence, with significant experience of dealing with the challenges of deprivation and social exclusion. Through the ICRC their opinions can be heard.

... The Faith communities command resources – people, networks, organisations, buildings – of great potential for regeneration and neighbourhood renewal.

... They also have an important and distinctive role in the voluntary and community sector, crucial in the provision of local and neighbourhood services in areas of long term disadvantage.
(www.neighbourhood.gov.uk/faith_communities.asp)

More recently, the development of government partnerships with Faith communities has become consolidated within the Home Office and its Cohesion and Faiths Unit within the Race, Cohesion and Faith Directorate. The government's interest in working with Faith organisations was reaffirmed by this department in its *Working together* report (Home Office, 2004). These central departments have encouraged and sponsored the involvement of Faith communities at local and regional level and in a range of initiatives and partnerships. There are advanced plans to combine the work of the ICRC and the Working Together Steering Group in a new Faith Communities Consultative Council, managed jointly by the ODPM and the Home Office.

It is clear, therefore, that the UK government has identified 'Faith communities' as potentially key 'containers' of social capital in achieving its targets for urban regeneration, social inclusion and community cohesion. How far is this faith in 'Faith' justified? And how far are the social networks and social capital of Faith groups understood or misunderstood by this official agenda?

Faith and social engagement

The scale and range of social engagement, broadly defined, by Faith groups and organisations is substantial and often unrecognised. Research evidence here has accumulated steadily in recent years.

One of the largest and most inclusive of studies in this field surveyed more than 2,300 Faith communities, encompassing nine religions (and, within this, nine Christian traditions) in north-west England (Northwest Development Agency, 2003). This research identified more than 5,000 significant 'non-worship' projects involving over 45,000 volunteers across the region. The projects addressed a wide range of issues and user groups:

... homelessness, racism, crime, drug and alcohol abuse, health, skills development, art, music, and environmental improvements. Across the survey results it was particularly evident that Faith communities are extensively involved in providing services for older people, children and more deprived neighbourhoods in the region ... Faith communities can help those working for regeneration, social inclusion or sustainable development to reach out to many of those who could be defined as 'hard to reach'....
(Northwest Development Agency, 2003, p 4)

Parallel studies in other regions have produced similar findings and statistics (see, for example, Yorkshire Churches, 2002, and Lovatt et al, 2005).

More recently, researchers in this field have begun to make explicit reference to the concept of 'social capital'. A study commissioned by the Anglican Diocese of Birmingham and supported by the Home Office concluded that the sampled church-organised projects can play 'a crucial role' in building social capital and social cohesion (Cairns et al, 2005, p 6). In a rather different context, a study commissioned by the Church of Scotland found that '[Church of Scotland] congregations make important contributions to the institutional infrastructure and social cohesion of many Scottish communities' (Flint and Kearns, 2004, p 18).

But such studies also underline the dangers of the celebratory tone of some official policy documents and Faith-commissioned research. Both reports stress that Faith communities face important internal and external obstacles in fulfilling any potential that they might have as sources and generators of social capital. They may themselves also *be* obstacles to the development of outward-looking and enriching social networks (see also Farnell et al, 2003). Moreover, incorporation within secular governance may serve to undermine the energy and distinctiveness of Faith-related networks and enterprise.

Aims of the research

Within this broad field, therefore, this research addresses a specific question that emerges from existing work:

- *How far can Faith organisations and their members contribute to social capital that not only bonds people together, but also enables them to cross boundaries and build bridges and links with others in civil society?*

The exploration of this question is designed to contribute to policy and practice by:

- critically assessing the prevalent association of 'Faith' with close-knit 'community' by exploring the extent to which Faith organisations enable or prevent people from moving beyond the 'thick' bonding of close local communities to a 'thinner' but more connected civic life;
- extending the understanding that derives from an association of Faith with 'neighbourhood' by shedding light on Faith-based activity beyond the local level;
- exploring Faith-based activities that lie outside official policy agendas, yet that also contribute to community cohesion and the wider strengthening of an associational public domain; and
- identifying good and problematic practice and key lessons for secular and Faith-based networks.

About the study

Our research aims are addressed and explored through a review of existing secondary evidence that serves to inform the primary field work. In addition to a review of existing literature, four members of the research group have made specific contributions as consultants[2] by drawing on their personal experience, knowledge and practical engagement to produce reviews of specific 'activity fields' in which Faith groups and their members are working with others in contexts and projects relevant to our research questions. This existing literature and evidence has then been used to inform and focus the primary fieldwork undertaken in the second part of the project period. Thus, within our main 'activity fields' we have explored more deeply the social capital constituted by Faith communities through focusing on specific initiatives, informal meeting places and particular 'episodes' that may illustrate or embody connecting social capital and/or exemplify the obstacles in building bridges and making links with other people, organisations and institutions. The research includes projects and activities stemming from Christian (including Black-majority), Hindu, Jewish, Muslim and Sikh organisations and their individual members. In some places we have made reference to particular organisations, but elsewhere we have maintained organisational anonymity. Further details of the research design and the methods of primary research are presented in Appendices A, B and C.

It is important to recognise one further issue. The 'Notes on the research group' above (pp viii-ix) confirm that the researchers are all variously committed to a Faith. This raises the prospect of a bias in favour of Faith communities as positive sources of social capital. Each reader will form a personal judgement on our success in achieving an accurate analysis that identifies both the strengths and the weaknesses of Faith organisations and their members in this context. One important counter to bias has been the composition of the Project Advisory Group, which included strongly engaged members with no religious faith as well as

---

2 Catherine Howarth, Dilwar Hussain, Sharon Palmer and Guy Wilkinson.

others from a variety of faith traditions. It might be added also that involvement in a Faith is for many a decidedly mixed experience. It can be a place of all kinds of enriching connections, but it can also afford a grandstand view of the more negative and divisive aspects of religion.

Report structure

The remaining chapters are organised in a particular sequence. Chapter 2 establishes a foundation for the later substantive chapters by assessing, first, the usefulness of social capital as a guiding idea in exploring the resources embedded in social networks and, second, the potential of Faith as a means of connection and a source of division. Chapter 3 draws upon a wider study (Archbishops' Council of the Church of England, 2004 – www. core.Anglican.org/info/interfaith/presence.pdf) to review the implications of bridging and linking social capital of often unrecognised or unknown geographical, organisational and learning frameworks of inter Faith, multi Faith, 'within-Faith', and Faith-secular encounter.

The next four chapters explore the extent of the 'connecting' and 'dividing' social capital stemming from 'Faith' by focusing, in turn, on places, people and participation. Chapter 4 examines the development and potential of Faith buildings as places and spaces of connection and the generation of trust. Chapter 5 looks 'behind' the buildings to the people and to the patterns of Faith association and organisation that may promote or inhibit the forging of connections across boundaries. Chapters 6 and 7 are concerned with the dynamic processes of participation and the evidence of social capital contributed by Faith individuals, networks and organisations in two contexts: participation in state-sponsored local governance; and participation in the networks and activities of a 'public domain', more independent of state and market. Finally, Chapter 8 draws on the research evidence to present the main conclusions and identify some implications for policy and practice.

Exploring 'social capital' and 'Faith'

We have noted the controversies surrounding both the idea of social capital and the contribution of Faith to human welfare. This chapter explores both debates a little further. First, we note the criticisms of the concept of 'social capital' but conclude that it can help us to sharpen our exploration of social networks and their positive and negative possibilities. We then turn to assess faith as a source of both connection and division between people. Religion can be an expression of 'negative social capital' but it may also prompt much more positive outcomes. This critical analysis is used in subsequent chapters to shape the field work that forms the basis for the remaining substantive chapters.

The idea of 'social capital'

The concept of 'social capital' has provoked an 'explosion of interest' since the mid-1990s (PIU, 2002, p 9). Field offers this explanation of the idea:

> The theory of social capital is, at heart, most straightforward. Its central thesis can be summed up in two words: *relationships matter*. By making connections with one another, and keeping them going over time, people are able to work together to achieve things that they either could not achieve by themselves, or could only achieve with great difficulty. People connect through a series of networks and they tend to share common values with other members of these networks; to the extent that these networks constitute a resource, they can be seen

as forming a kind of capital. (Field, 2003, p 1 – emphasis added)

A recurring theme here is 'trust' which can be both a cause and a consequence of social capital. On the one hand, existing trust may prompt the formation or further development of networks. On the other, where networks are sustained and people find that they are developing some common understandings and values so that they can rely upon each other, trust emerges. Reviewing the literature, therefore, Gilchrist (2004, p 4) finds social capital broadly defined as 'a collective asset made up of social networks based on shared norms and trust and mutuality'. But social capital is also a 'contested and problematic concept' (Taylor, 2000, p 1026). Four of the common objections are reviewed briefly here.

A disturbing language?

There is sometimes uneasiness at the application of the instrumental 'economic' language of 'capital' in the context of (often informal) social networks and community development. Rational choice theory informs the influential work of both James Coleman (1988-89, 1994) and Nan Lin (2001). Its basic assumption is that people act rationally to maximise their benefits and minimise their costs when they choose alternative courses of action so as to get the best outcomes according to their own preferences. This jars with many for whom the emphasis on 'capital' seems to limit action and debate to the parameters of capitalist relations (Field, 2003). In particular this challenges the language of religious faith and the subordination of self-interest within the worship of the divine and a related ethic of service to others.

However, rational choice theory itself accepts that people's optimising behaviour may be directed by altruistic principles, stemming from religious or non-religious understandings and experiences. Also if capital is indeed 'captured through social relations' and 'relationships matter', then traditional narrow, individualist understandings of the sources of human well-being are confronted by the idea of 'social capital'.

An ideological tramline?

Second, the idea of social capital is associated with a political philosophy – moral communitarianism – that many reject. Robert Putnam's work in the US has been particularly influential (Putnam, 1995, 2000; Putnam and Feldstein, 2003) and has influenced the social and regeneration strategies of New Labour (Levitas, 1998). Putnam has defined social capital in terms similar to those used later by Gilchrist (see above) and others. However, his work often has a nostalgic and consensual tone and his substantive emphasis is on revived voluntary organisations and the acceptance of civic volunteering responsibilities as the means to reverse the decline in social capital and growing 'civic deficit' that he perceives in the US. New Labour has also stressed personal and civic responsibility and the role of voluntary (including Faith) organisations in achieving greater 'social cohesion', sharing with Putnam an emphasis on the social capital embedded in 'legitimate' voluntary and community organisations as a source of social stability.

A forthright expression of this essentially consensual definition of social capital is found in a practitioner 'toolkit' developed by the UK government's Neighbourhood Renewal Unit (NRU): 'Social capital is the 'social glue' between people, organisations and communities that enables them to work together to pursue shared objectives' (www.renewal.net). This 'social glue' definition provokes the suspicion that social capital is a concept that shifts responsibility for social exclusion on to poor people and poor places; that it acts as a cover for cuts in social welfare and operates to draw the representatives of 'recognised' voluntary and community organisations into 'partnerships' in which inequalities of power and resources and the presence of conflict are papered over.

This understanding of social capital must not be reflected uncritically in this research. An emphasis on traditional voluntary organisations can lead to a neglect of emerging new forms of social capital. In a context of decline in some formal religious traditions, we must not miss emerging informal and less hierarchical expressions of religious social engagement and newer forms of association and affiliation. Faith-based projects and Faith buildings are not always what they seem to outsiders. They may provide places and spaces where people 'negotiate difference' and 'transgress' the normal boundaries of interaction (Amin, 2002). We have found examples of 'Faith as social capital' in 'legitimate' civil society but we have also encountered examples and episodes of social capital in more informal Faith settings. Moreover, the complexity and diversity of 'religion' is such that we should expect to find that social capital can act as a source of social retreat or active resistance and critique, not simply as an instrument of 'governability' (Furbey and Macey, 2005).

This recognition of the non-traditional, informal and non-consensual qualities of some Faith-related social capital encourages a focus on inequalities within Faith communities and particularly on gender and age as dimensions of social capital formation. Where men and older people often dominate formal positions and determine priorities, can the idea of social capital be used critically to explore the present significance and future potential of the (often less visible) activity of women and young people as builders of connections and links?

Putnam's emphasis on voluntary organisations as carriers of social capital can lead us to neglect, not only informal activity, but also, at the opposite pole, 'the influence of state and commercial institutions in shaping the context of associational activity, and hence the form of social capital' (Stoker et al, 2004, p 390). Might the co-option of Faith networks and organisations as 'social glue' be corrosive of their social capital?

Accentuating the positive – neglecting the negative?

Although 'social capital' tends to be a honeyed term, Taylor reminds us that it can be 'a negative force' (Taylor, 2000, p 1027). Like another positively charged concept – 'community' – social capital has a 'dark side'. Gilchrist's list of the problems associated with close-knit community can also be applied to 'social capital'. The social capital embedded in social networks can be:

- exclusive of others
- a perpetuator of stereotypes of 'outsiders'
- tribalist and oppressive to members
- punitive to deviants
- an inhibitor of new knowledge
- a source of stagnation and isolation
- a source of internal inequality (cf Gilchrist, 2004, p 9).

Such destructive social capital can be identified in networks of both the rich and the poor. For example, Pierre Bourdieu stresses the cultural power of elite networks (Bourdieu, 1986). In current policy, destructive social capital is associated much more with criminal networks in poor districts or with ethnic and religious minorities seen as living lives 'parallel' to others (Cantle, 2001). There is recognition of the 'downside' of social capital in government (PIU, 2002, pp 31-3). However, official action is concentrated on poorer places and people.

Recent world and domestic British events have underlined the ability of 'religion' to express many of the features of negative social capital and to express them in a particularly enduring, damaging and intractable way. This is an important issue for the present research to which we return later.

A new name for old concerns?

Finally, the apparent novelty of the concept of social capital is challenged. Does it enable us to develop genuinely new insights on social life to inform new and effective social policy? Or is it simply a flimsy new cover for the perennial sociological debate on social order and concerns regarding 'community'? Certainly the indiscriminate use of 'social capital' risks rendering the concept meaningless by becoming everything to everyone (Fine, 1999). Yet the exploration of the capital embedded in social networks may enable us to 'go in closer' in exploring issues of community development and empowerment. This view is encouraged as we turn now to explore the interesting degree of consensus that has emerged regarding the key types of social capital.

Types of social capital – bonding, bridging and linking

Many researchers have found helpful Woolcock's distinction between three types of social capital (Woolcock, 2001). In her exploration of the 'well-connected community', Gilchrist expresses the three types in these terms:

- Bonding
  based on enduring, multi-faceted relationships between similar people with strong mutual commitments such as among friends, family and other close-knit groups.

- Bridging
  formed from the connections between people who have less in common, but may have overlapping interests, for example, between neighbours, colleagues, or between different groups within a community.

- Linking
  derived from the links between people or organisations beyond peer boundaries, cutting across status and similarity and enabling people to exert influence and reach resources outside their normal circles (Gilchrist, 2004, p 6).

Gilchrist argues that *all* these types of social capital are needed to produce the well-connected community. Socially 'rich' people are those with relationships that 'bond', 'bridge' and 'link'. Thus, the *horizontal* relationships of bonding (with family and close friends) and bridging (with other community groups) need to be supplemented by *vertical* relationships (with those with a different 'knowledge' and other resources, including government).

A related distinction is that between 'strong ties' and 'weak ties' (Granovetter, 1973). Strong ties equate broadly to 'bonding' social capital where we are engaged in dense social networks composed of people like ourselves in terms of resources of wealth, reputation, power or lifestyle (Lin, 2001, p 47), or in terms of shared past lives and common sentiments that produce 'a repository of 'common sense' and local knowledge, acting as a source of wisdom, information and 'gossip' (Gilchrist, 2004, p 8).

Weak ties equate broadly to 'bridging' and 'linking' social capital. Here, we are engaged in less dense networks and in less frequent interactions with people with whom we have less in common. We may come together on the basis of shared problems (for example, concerns over neighbourhood crime) or shared opportunities (invitations to join a regeneration partnership board). We are dealing here with people who we otherwise experience as in some degree 'different' from ourselves. The exercise involves making 'bridges' and developing trust in more restricted encounters than those obtaining in the context of close 'bonding'. In terms of 'linking', a further set of weak ties is developed when links are formed between people with different levels of power or status (for example, when representatives of poor communities engage with the local or national political elite).

The phrase 'weak ties' may suggest that 'bridging' and 'linking' social capital are less significant for people and communities than 'bonding' social capital. Certainly, our sense of identity, and the confidence that we need to move out into the wider world, derives substantially from our relationships with people close to ourselves and with whom we share some similarity. Hence, 'bonding' social capital is an essential basis from which we can begin the more difficult project of 'moving out' and relating to people who are unlike ourselves. But, if we derive our social capital simply from within our own circle, we cut ourselves off from the wider experiences and resources needed to maximise our social capital. Thus, 'systems with low levels of connectivity and high homogeneity ... become stagnant, because they are unable to adapt' (Taylor, 2000, p 1032).

As with all typologies and distinctions, caution is needed. In the particular context of 'Faith', what appears from the outside to be a 'bonded' community of shared sentiment and strong internal ties may be a more complex gathering of people who experience many of the other members as 'different' and the task of 'bridging' as both important and difficult. Conversely, work 'across' the community in campaigns that initially involve 'bridging' and weak ties that are largely instrumental and devoid of sentiment, or 'linking' experiences in official regeneration partnerships, may develop into much closer forms of attachment and trust

Nevertheless, this research reflects our view that the 'bonding–bridging–linking' typology and related distinctions provide a useful framework to assess the extent and the ways in which Faith organisations and their members move beyond 'bonding' to the demanding task of building the connections of 'bridging' and 'linking'.

Faith and connection

All the major Faith traditions encompassed by this research have core principles that can motivate bridge-building and link-making through community service, cooperation, peace-making, the pursuit of social justice, and the acceptance of others. There is a major danger here, of course, in oversimplifying the complex and in finding similarities where, despite the use of the same *words*, different *meanings* remain. Nevertheless, we follow here Oliver McTernan who concludes that, despite their significant differences in thought and practice, there are 'important resemblances in belief that exist between the mainstream world religions' so that:

> In each faith tradition we see an affirmation of life that extends beyond the physical boundaries of their own communities. We recognize also an inherent respect for individual choices and the acknowledgement that there should be no coercion in matters of religion, a precept based on the belief that faith rests essentially on the freedom of the individual to say yes or no to what is proposed as truth. In each tradition, crossing the boundaries

of culture and ethnicity, there is clearly a seminal presence of the right of the individual both to seek truth and to dissent – principles that lie right at the very heart of the Universal Declaration of Human Rights. (McTernan, 2003, p 148)

Specifically, therefore, the three monotheistic Abrahamic Faiths – Judaism, Christianity and Islam – all enjoin the worship of one God of justice and mercy who requires a human commitment to these same qualities. Within the Judaic tradition, from the earliest Hebrew scriptures, it is possible to detect a changing understanding from a God as belonging to a particular people, sometimes with the attributes of an ancient tribal deity, to a more expansive and inclusive vision of a God who prompts concern for the oppressed and work for the well-being of all people as bearers of the 'image of God' (Ward, 2004, pp 118-22).

In Christianity, this is expressed in Christ's distillation of the law into love for God and love for neighbours, the latter not confined to people 'like us' next door, but extended to the presently feared and reviled Samaritan stranger 'over the wall'. For Christians, Christ is the fullest expression of God as forgiving and loving, the infinite embracing finite human experience in the cause of reconciliation, demonstrating in the process the infinite value of all people, the sanctity of the material world and human obligation to work inclusively for the common good.

Islam does not share the Christian belief in the incarnation of God. But it holds as a central principle the 'oneness' of humanity and shares with Christianity an understanding of God as compassionate and merciful and the obligation of believers as free moral agents to work for peace and justice. Regarding peace, the Qur'an rejects conversion by force, insisting that there be no compulsion in religion (Qur'an 22:256). And, in terms of justice, *zakat*, the paying of alms (or charity) tax to benefit the poor, is one of the Five Pillars of Islam. This expresses the wider Islamic belief in the harmony between the spiritual and the material and individual and collective responsibility to strive (*jihad*) to submit to the will of God in the care of creation. How far does Islam encourage the 'boundary-crossing' that is the focus of this

research? It is true that a binary distinction has commonly been made between the *dar al-Islam* (abode of Islam) and the *dar al-harb* (abode of war) – the world of Islam and the world of others. The *ummah* constitutes a community of specifically Muslim faith. However, the Qur'an also refers to a wider community, *qawmi* ('my people'), which involves a fraternal relationship between Muslims and other people, regardless of their beliefs, and a wider respect for diversity endorsed by the Prophet (see Hussain, 2004) thus: 'O mankind! Behold, We have created you from a male and a female, and have made you nations and tribes, so that you might come to know one another....' (Qur-an 49:13).

A fundamental tenet for Sikhs is the essential unity of humanity and the equality of all people before God. Through personal and collective perseverance, Sikhs are expected to develop in honesty, compassion, generosity, patience and humility. There is a principle of care and service to others, whatever their religion, and an emphasis on combining action and belief. The practice of *kar-sewa* involves selfless voluntary service for religious activities. A daily prayer for Sikhs is: 'By Thy Grace may everybody be blessed in the world'.

Generalisation is especially difficult in the case of Hinduism, which, even more than other Faiths, is not a unified tradition. However, Hinduism upholds 'the divine qualities of forgiveness, compassion, the absence of anger and malice, peace and harmlessness' (McTernan, 2003, pp 45-6). It sees the world as having 'a common ancestry' (McTernan, 2003, p 133) and the one ultimate reality, *Brahman*, as including 'all the diversity of the cosmos as part of itself' (Ward, 2004, p 134). Material selfishness stands as a barrier to the ultimate reality and freedom from suffering. The teachings of *dharma* are that the bliss of enlightenment is reached by valuing all beings more than ourselves, particularly through the difficult process of cherishing strangers, who do not immediately seem so important to our happiness compared with family and friends. Ghandi challenged the spiritual sanction given by Hindu tradition for the divisions and inequalities of untouchability. He absorbed elements of Christianity and Islam into his own Hindu life (Zaehner, 1962), seeing the essence of Hinduism as being captured in an

Upanishad scripture verse that has been paraphrased as saying:

> God is the Lord who pervades the whole universe and all of it is his. Therefore, you must renounce the world because it is not yours and then enjoy and work in it because it is his and he wishes you to co-operate with him in the destruction of evil. (Zaehner, 1962, p 181)

This brief sketch indicates some important common ground amidst the continuing major differences. All have commitments to peace, justice, honesty, service, personal responsibility and forgiveness that can contribute to the development of networks and the trusting relationships which characterise positive social capital. In particular, all Faith traditions contain the hope and possibility of tolerance, and indeed a *respect* and obligation to 'the other', suggesting potential for a contribution to 'bridging' and 'linking' social capital.

Yet we must also recognise that religion can be a powerful source of division. Drawing on his experience in conflict resolution in different parts of the world, McTernan recognises that 'competing claims on the exclusivity or superiority of one interpretation of truth over the other have often led to abandonment or outright violation of these ['connecting'] principles' (McTernan, 2003, p 148). Expressed in the starkest terms: 'There is brutal, callous, intolerant religion and there is compassionate, kind and tolerant religion' (Ward, 2004, p 121).

Faith and division

The divisiveness of religion is given ultimate expression in physical violence. But Faith communities can also be characterised by other powerful forms of disconnection from other groups or wider society. Hence, while some groups and their individual members are prompted by their beliefs to engage across religious and Faith–secular boundaries and to participate in wider civil society and processes of governance, others understand their Faith as requiring segregation from other religious traditions and secular culture. Religious understandings that require a strong boundary

from the rest of 'the world' can produce a passive retreat or a more active (and sometimes destructive) assertion of distinctiveness. Ruthven contrasts introverted and isolationist sects with more challenging religious movements that are more prone to 'fight back' against the pluralist secular world: 'For the active fundamentalist (as distinct from the passive traditionalist) the quest for salvation cannot be realised by withdrawing into a cultural enclave' (Ruthven, 2004, p 57).

Inter Faith or Faith–secular tensions and conflicts are often seen as caused by other, 'deeper', economic, social, political or cultural factors. Such explanations flow from the still-dominant analyses of religion in social science. Interestingly, they can also be attractive to religious leaders as they help to let religion 'off the hook'. The relative importance of various factors – including religion – in interpreting violence and social division is a continuing and unresolved controversy. However, religion has been prominent in many of the conflicts of the post-Cold War era. Reviewing the Arab–Israeli dispute, Ruthven, as a secular commentator, concluded that: 'It is the religious factor, not the conflict of interests that threatens to prevent a settlement' (Ruthven, 2004, p 3). Similarly, McTernan, a Catholic priest, reviews a series of world conflicts in which religion is a 'presenting' source of conflict. He concludes that 'Whatever the psychological, social and political factors that trigger violence in fringe or mainstream religious bodies, the religious mindset is itself an important factor that needs to be acknowledged and understood if durable solutions are to be found for many current conflicts' (McTernan, 2003, p 40).

Hence, although all religions aspire to peace, all have at various times sanctioned intolerance, segregation and violence, as reflected in the long history of bloody religious wars and in recent or contemporary conflicts such as those in Northern Ireland, the Balkans, Palestine, Kashmir and Sri Lanka.

Far from fading away, religion may be displacing some secular ideologies as a source of motivation and identity (Ruthven, 2004, pp 4-5), and thus as a source of both cohesion and conflict. Globalisation and its associated migration and cultural pluralism produces opportunity and enrichment but also anxiety.

The secular and the religious encounter one another with a new sharpness, while religions that had lived at a distance from one another are often together on the same street or looking at each other over the same wall. In what he calls this increasingly 'liquid' world with less fixed points, Zygmunt Bauman has identified 'a constant threat to social integration – and also to the feeling of individual security and self-assurance' (Bauman, 2004, p 82). These anxieties provoke a search for security and certainty in a world of fewer fixed points.

This search for what Bauman terms a 'haven' by 'hapless sailors' (Bauman, 2004, p 46) on a threatening sea may find secular expression, for example, in lifestyles that place a premium on 'house-as-haven', with affluent gated communities the ultimate expression. Or it may be seen in racist politics and forms of community mobilisation and defence that serve to remove ambiguity and shut out 'difference'. But such times are also likely to provoke a religious response for, although this does not by any means exhaust its definition, religion has always offered a shield against chaos. As we assess the potential of Faith communities as a source of 'connecting' social capital, therefore, we must recognise this powerful counter-current.

'Fundamentalism' was a term first coined in relation to a call within American Protestantism for a return to the 'fundamentals' of Faith in the face of science and liberal secularism. The applicability of the term 'fundamentalist' to traditions within other world religions or, further, to secular perspectives, is an issue of debate. Ruthven argues that there are 'family resemblances' between fast-growing movements within most of the major world Faiths. He describes such movements as 'a 'religious way of being' that manifests itself in a strategy by which beleaguered believers attempt to preserve their distinctive identity as a people or group in the face of modernity and secularization' (Ruthven, 2003, p 8). This sense of embattlement is compounded by the increasing exposure of Faiths to *each other* as religions. This can reinforce the retreat into certainty and the dominance of rigid theologies, understandings and practices.

This discussion suggests that we must expect a diversity of religious contributions to connecting social capital, with some contributing little or indeed negatively. However, the following chapters focus on situations and initiatives that seem to offer, at least at first sight, positive potential as contexts and vehicles for connecting social capital. Meanwhile, we are alerted to the negative possibilities.

3

Frameworks for Faith

This chapter reviews three frameworks – geographic, organisational and learning – within which Faith communities have developed various forms of social capital. These frameworks are often not very visible beyond those who work within them and their significance is therefore sometimes not fully understood or appreciated by commentators. Subsequent chapters offer deeper analysis, illustrated by a range of particular case studies. The wider perspective of this chapter provides an important initial overview of the differing development of the Faith communities in providing frameworks for social capital.

Geographic frameworks

The formation of bridging and linking social capital is strongly influenced by the numerical size of the Faith communities; their diversity in ethnic, linguistic, cultural and religious terms; and particularly their geographic concentration or dispersion. These are the raw materials available to build social capital. The fewer the communities, the lesser their diversity, or the more limited their geographic dispersion, the lower is the potential for the formation of social capital in general and for bridging and linking forms in particular.

The evidence shows that, as the more recently established Faith communities have grown, diversified and extended, so there has been a corresponding growth in social capital formation. Not surprisingly in the early stages of the formation of communities, bonding relationships were paramount. As a sense of a more permanent residence and belonging developed, so again bonding capital was reinforced, particularly with the establishment of places of worship as centres of religious and communal life. The formation from this time of relationships with the pre-existing religious communities (primarily Christian, but also Jewish) has led to the development of bridging forms of social capital (although we must underline here the cold reception accorded by many White churches to Black Christians from the Caribbean and the subsequent development of Black-majority churches outside the 'mainstream' denominations). With the development of significant public-sector urban renewal and regeneration policies and a strong emphasis by government on the role of Faith communities, linking forms of capital have also started to develop.

The 2001 Census provided a baseline indicator of the numbers of people choosing to identify themselves in terms of a Faith. The geographic distributions of the Faith communities in relation to each other revealed by the Census are of particular interest. These data are normally published on a ward basis, although there are more detailed 'super output area' data now available. However, there is a set of data, approximating to 'neighbourhood', which provides a systematic small-scale geographic analysis across England. This derives from the reallocation of the Census information to the 13,000 ecclesiastical parishes of the Church of England and provides a systematic, detailed geographic picture of the distribution of Faith allegiance. This shows that just under 80% of all parishes/neighbourhoods in England have some proportion of their population as people of Faiths other than Christian. The distribution is given in Table 1 below.

Closer analysis indicates the extent to which people of different Faiths actually co-exist geographically with each other. We find a varied picture, both as between different groupings of Faith communities and as between different areas in England. The data tend to confirm that there is a significant degree of neighbourhood separation and of

Table 1: Proportion of Faiths other than Christian by Church of England parishes

% other Faiths	Number of parishes	% all parishes
> 0 to 1	4,371	36.6
> 1 to 5	3,624	29.5
> 5 to 10	637	5.2
> 10 to 25	554	4.5
> 25 to 50	227	1.9
> 50	61	0.5
Total	9,474	
Total all parishes	12,264	78.2

'parallel lives' as between Faith communities. This raises significant questions for their ability to create bridging forms of social capital. The data have been assembled on the basis of the 44 dioceses of the Church of England, which comprise a mix of mainly urban, mixed and mainly rural contexts.

The following figures for four different dioceses indicate the widely different patterns between them. For each diocesan area they show the religious composition of each parish where more than 10% of the population are of Faiths other than Christian. The figures indicate the extent to which different Faith communities are geographically associated with each other in quite local neighbourhoods. The substantially differing patterns of association between different areas are relevant to our research. Blackburn provides an example of the essentially bipolar communities of the Northern cities. Birmingham appears to be

more mixed but, on the ground, the Muslim communities are strongly concentrated in the east side of the city in the wards of Saltley, Sparkbook, Small Heath and Sparkhill. The Hindu and Sikh communities by contrast are largely located in the western areas around Smethwick. In St Albans and Chelmsford we find more mixed communities, although there remains strong differentiation. Across the four areas – and across the other diocesan areas – there is a similar pattern. Sikh and Hindu communities associate geographically with each other; those identifying themselves as Christian are present in all neighbourhoods; Jewish and Muslim communities generally do not inhabit the same neighbourhoods, but Jewish communities are associated with Sikh and Hindu communities; and, in turn, these latter communities tend to be located apart from the Muslim communities.

There are further consequences for the formation of social capital associated with these geographical patterns, particularly, for example, in relation to schools. For primary schools, neighbourhood is normally the main criterion in admissions policies. To the extent that particular Faith communities are associated with particular neighbourhoods, the pupil population of the school will mirror that association. For secondary schools, the pattern can be different, particularly where pupils from Faith communities travel from their residential neighbourhoods to adjacent ones with different religious compositions.

Figure 1: Birmingham Faith communities by parish

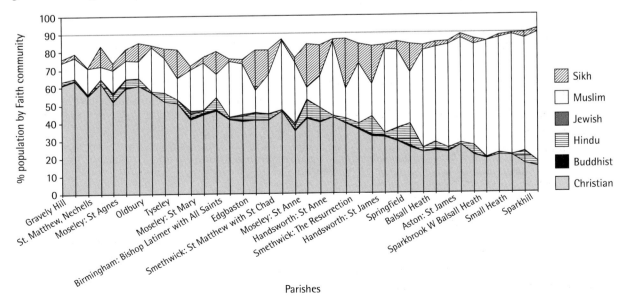

Figure 2: Chelmsford Faith communities by parish

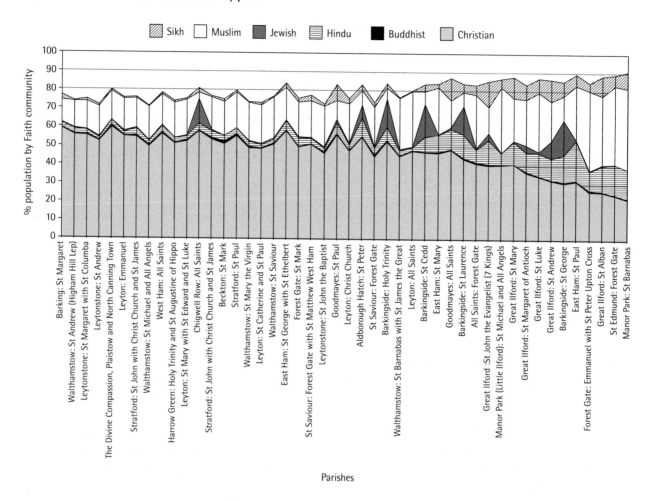

Figure 3: Blackburn Faith communities by parish

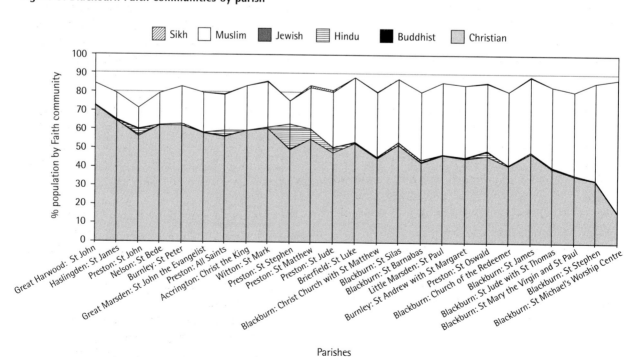

Figure 4: St Albans Faith communities by parish

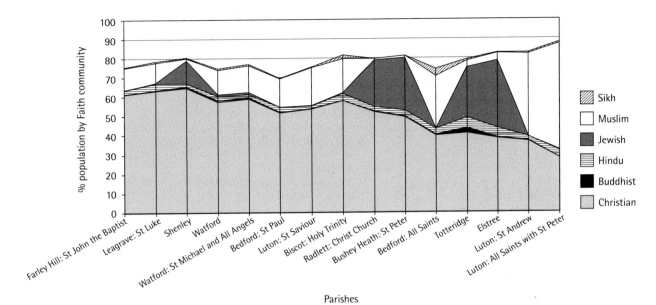

The significance of these data lies in the challenge they pose to those Faith communities not usually geographically proximate to bridge and link to one another. The remainder of this chapter examines the extent to which the development of organisational frameworks for encounter is compensating for the limited extent of geographical encounter.

Organisational frameworks

One of the strongest indicators of increasing bridging and linking social capital has been the rapid growth of formal and informal associational structures within and between Faith communities and the increasing connections with wider civil society.

The internal structures of the different Faith communities vary considerably in scale and depth. This is not simply a matter of the longevity, size or organisational ability of different Faith communities. It is related also to more fundamental theological and historical factors. Islam's self-understanding, for example, does not lead to the formalised structures common in much of Christianity. Nor, beyond the few Islamic states, does it possess central religious administrative structures in the ways that the larger Christian churches in the West have developed.

Of particular interest for this research are the structures of engagement that cross the boundaries of Faith communities and the frameworks of connection with the non-religious elements of civil society. These operate formally and informally and at national, regional and local levels.

Nationally, there are multilateral and bilateral structures. Examples of the multilateral include the Inter Faith Network for the United Kingdom, which has constructed a substantial membership network with associated representational and consultative structures; the Inner Cities Religious Council, formed as part of the follow up to the 'Faith in the City' report (ACUPA, 1985), which links the leadership of the Faith communities to official and political structures; and (of more recent development), the Faith-based Regeneration Network, formed from nine Faith traditions by and for regeneration practitioners who identify with Faith traditions, or who work with or for Faith community organisations.

There is also a growing range of formal bilateral organisations. At the national level, the Council of Christians and Jews was the first such organisation, formed in 1942. More recently, and still to be fully launched, is the national Christian Muslim Forum. Less developed and located on a spectrum between the formal and informal, are a range of discussion groups for Muslims and Jews,

Hindus and Muslims, Christians and Hindus and others. These include organisations such as the Three Faiths Forum, which brings together the three 'Abrahamic' Faiths.

At the regional and local levels there are representational structures that link Faith communities to the structures of government at regional and local authority levels. These include, for example, the seats for Faith community representatives on the regional assemblies and on the Local Strategic Partnerships. At the local level there has been a burgeoning of Faith forums and councils and the Inter Faith Network Directory (www.theredirectory.org.uk/orgs/ifnuk.html) records some 185 of these, many having come into existence since 11 September 2001.

In addition to the formal structures for bridging and linking, there is also a series of more informal arrangements between Faith community leaders at local and national levels, which play an important, largely hidden, part in developing the structures of trust that need to precede and underlie the development of formal organisations. At the micro level there is a dense network of friendship arrangements across Faith communities through informal associations for discussion, dialogue and action.

This brief examination of organisational frameworks indicates that although the formation of bonding capital is indeed significant, structural arrangements that bridge between Faith communities and link them to wider society are developing strongly. Fuller discussion and examples of Faith associational and organisational 'spaces' are developed in Chapter 5.

Learning frameworks

We have shown that there is an extensive geographic dispersion of religiously identifying people and communities, and that this is an important precondition for the development of social capital. We have also shown that there has been a substantial growth in the range of organisational arrangements within and between Faith communities and between 'Faith' and wider society. A key issue will be the nature and strength of the *motivations* to

encourage or limit the formation of bridging and linking structures and relations. Economic factors are of key importance in facilitating geographic dispersion or neighbourhood segregation. The more that members of minority Faith communities are included in the wider processes of wealth creation, the greater will be the motivation for dispersion and geographic integration. The greater the security and xenophobic anxieties of society, the more separation and internally bonding forms of social capital will be encouraged. Other motivational forces lie in government attitudes and policies towards Faith communities and in society's attitudes to religion and 'race' generally.

The impacts of these motivational forces are themselves dependent upon the knowledge, understanding and attitudes of the various actors towards each other. An important consideration here is the strength and flexibility of the educational frameworks that assist members of Faith communities to understand and appreciate each other. Furthermore, what opportunities are there for people in wider secular society and leadership to understand and appreciate the attitudes and contributions of members of Faith communities? An assessment of the nature and strength of Faith education will be an important element in understanding the ways in which the formation of bridging and linking social capital will develop. Only a few indications can be provided here, but the learning frameworks within which motivation is created for bridging and linking are a key concern for further research.

Much has been written about religious education in community and voluntary schools and about the positive and negative effects of religious ethos schools in relation to mutual understanding and social cohesion. It is not possible to explore the full range of arguments around Faith schools here. However, in this section we look briefly at developments in educational structures, formal and informal, which in themselves represent the formation of bridging and linking capital and which tend to provide the motivation for further forms of association across Faith communities and other social, economic and political groups. We introduce here specific illustrative examples found in three contexts: within particular Faith communities; across Faith and other communities; and academic provision.

Learning within particular Faith communities

The primary educational concern of the more recently growing Faith communities in the UK has been to reinforce their own religions and teachings among their members and particularly their younger generations. The impact of wider Western culture on second and third generations has been profound and it is not surprising that the need to pass on the religious tradition effectively has been at the forefront of concern. Within each of the Faith communities there are now significant regional and national educational establishments. Of secondary importance has been the desire to teach about the nature and beliefs of other Faiths. Even where this is undertaken, it remains relatively uncommon to invite adherents of another Faith to expound their beliefs and practices. More frequently the beliefs and practices of other Faiths are seen through the eyes of a person of one's own Faith. However, two illustrative counter-examples can be detailed briefly here:

First, the Church of England, in association with other Christian churches, has moved to establish a series of national learning outcome statements as a foundation for initial and ongoing clergy training. These outcome statements explicitly include several requirements for clergy in relation to Faiths other than Christian. Clergy must be able to:

'• demonstrate ability to take a leading role in working with other partners, representing the church in public life and other institutions, and working with other faith leaders where possible.
• demonstrate growing awareness of, and reflective engagement with, beliefs, practices and spiritualities of other Faith traditions.
• demonstrate ability to develop and sustain dialogue with representatives of other faith traditions.' (Church of England – Ministry of the Archbishops' Council)

Second, within the Muslim communities, the Muslim College opens its prospectus with these

words: 'The Muslim College aims to implement its curriculum within an explicit acknowledgement that international society is multicultural, multi-ethnic, multi-lingual and multi-faith' (Muslim College website: www.muslimcollege.ac.uk).

Across Faith and other communities

Apart from the Religious Education curricula in schools, evidence for systematic educational programmes for adults cutting across Faith and other communities is less widely available and regular collaborative educational programmes sponsored or supported by the Faith communities seem less common. There are notable exceptions. In Leicester, for example, there is an important collaboration between Christian and Muslim communities through the Islamic Foundation and the St Philip's Centre. This is developing joint training courses for the formation and education of chaplains to prisons and hospitals and mutual understanding in other contexts. In West Yorkshire and in Leicester the Intercultural Communication and Leadership School has brokered continuing relationships between young adults of different communities. In London, the Citizens Organising Foundation has engaged across Faith and other communities in extensive social action and learning programmes (see Chapter 7).

Academic frameworks of Faith

Beyond the Faith communities themselves, there has been a burgeoning of centres for the study of religion at universities and a full study of these in relation to their impact on the formation of bridging and linking social capital would be of considerable interest. The expansion of such centres reflects the response of universities to the growing salience of religion in public life. The establishment of academic centres of research and teaching brings students and researchers of different Faith traditions into deep association with each other and with the wider structures and disciplines of the academy. Three different academic contexts can be distinguished: confessional centres for the study of particular religions; multi Faith centres; and centres specialising in inter Faith relations.

In several universities, centres have been formed that, to a greater or lesser extent, are formally associated with the university, but which have a clear confessional basis. In Oxford, the Oxford Centre for Islamic Studies and the Oxford Centre for Hindu Studies are clearly confessional organisations whose role is to provide teaching and research from their religious perspective, but within the disciplines of the academy. Both these centres are 'associated institutions of the university' and have formal teaching and other relations with university departments and colleges.

Multi Faith centres have a different role. For example, although part of the University, the Multi-Faith Centre at the University of Derby is a separately registered charity for staff and students of the university and the wider community. It acts as a resource to the university and well beyond. It includes MultiFaithNet (www.multifaithnet.org/ religions/Interfaith/index.asp), a self-access research, learning, information and dialogue tool, providing updated access to global electronic resources useful for the study of world religious traditions and the practice of inter Faith dialogue.

Finally, several university centres specialising in inter Faith relations have been established, focusing on two or more particular Faiths. Such centres tend to have significant staff members of the Faiths in question, but are formally part of the university structures and ethos. The University of London includes the Centre for Christianity and Interreligious Dialogue. Its aims and self-understanding are typical of this type of centre:

> The Centre for Christianity in Interreligious Dialogue exists to advance scholarship and dialogue, through research, teaching, conferences and publications. The Centre provides a forum for the study and practice of the encounter between Christianity and the other major religious traditions. The Centre's role is to promote an awareness and knowledge of the importance of interreligious engagement between the world's religious cultures and traditions. (The London School of Theology website: www.lst.ac.uk)

The University of Birmingham includes as part of its Department of Theology and Religion, the Centre for the Study of Islam and Christian–Muslim Relations (CSIC) as a joint Muslim–Christian graduate teaching and research institute. It describes itself as follows:

> A centre seeking to encourage respect for the various Christian and Muslim traditions in their own terms and rejects polemics and proselytism. With academic integrity, the programmes of the CSIC seek to give equal attention to the theoretical dimensions of Christian-Muslim relations and the lived situations of communities in plural contexts, and to understand the relationships between the two spheres. (University of Birmingham Department of Theology and Religion; Centre for the Study of Islam and Christian–Muslim Relations website: www.bham.ac.uk)

Summary

The aim of this chapter has been to demonstrate that there are extensive and dense frameworks within and across Faith communities and the wider community that are an important, if often not very visible, layer in the formation of social capital. These frameworks contribute substantially to bonding forms of capital, particularly so in the more recently established Faith communities. However, there are increasingly strong networks where the primary purpose is to bridge and link across the Faith communities.

4

People in places

The community life of most Faith groups focuses on a building. For some this is an historic building, for others it is newly built or an adaptation from another type of use. Increasingly, buildings that were once associated with one group are sold on to another religious group as the nature of the local population changes. These buildings also serve the social capital bonding needs of the community. They are safe spaces where people can come together to share a social life and meet many of their own needs. But they are often also much more.

This chapter considers the role of buildings and places in the formation and use of bridging and linking social capital. It uses four buildings as examples of where a bonded Faith group is also engaging in bridging and linking that is focused on the building: the Gujarat Hindu Society in Preston (GHS); St Mary's Anglican Church in Sheffield; the New Testament Church of God in Mile End, East London (NTCG); and St Peter's Church and Community Centre, Coventry. The first section examines the bridging and linking social capital focused on the building, and what it achieves. The second section looks at critical factors that have been important in the development of bridging and linking social capital. The final section analyses the barriers, difficulties and negative aspects that have been experienced.

Buildings in bridging and linking

The buildings in this study are all used for religious and social services to their own Faith communities. These activities also deliver a range of benefits to the neighbourhood that should not be lightly dismissed (Finneron and Dinham, 2002). However, the focus here is on the bridging and linking social capital that develops through the use of the buildings.

There are two main ways in which the bridging and linking is generated. First, the provision of services focused on the members of the Faith tradition can bring them into closer contact with the wider community and increase mutual understanding and trust. Second, the provision of services or facilities directly to the wider community can bring people together across the traditional divides of Faith and culture. This often brings individuals into association with wider forums or activity.

Service provision, buildings and social capital

This first characteristic is well demonstrated in the example of GHS in Preston. GHS has strongly developed services for the local Hindu community that also bring it into contact with wider society. In the 1970s, its youth group took the lead in coordinating communication with other Hindu youth groups around the UK to organise a national sporting event that has since become annual. Monthly health seminars led to the establishment of a Lancashire Gujarat Health Users Forum, made up of professionals and members of the community, to act as a catalyst with the mainstream agencies for the delivery of culturally sensitive services. During the 1990s, when unemployment rates were high, particularly among the Asian community, GHS accessed funding from a variety of statutory sources to provide a Learn Direct Centre offering training and advice. This came to be used also by members of the wider community.

Another example is found in the NTCG in Mile End. The NTCG has been using its presence and the resource of its building to create important links between the Black community and the police, for example with 'Adopt a Cop': 'That's simply where a local church adopts a police officer, prays for them, knows something about what they are doing, but also tries to encourage young people in our congregation to think about the police service as a career' (senior worker, NTCG). This has been successful and a number of the congregation are now police officers. The Metropolitan Police Authority is also a partner in the development of the Ascent Citizenship Centre, the planned next phase in the development of the building. The relationship with the church has also helped to lessen tension and mistrust by dispelling negative stereotypes:

> 'Because we have an open policy for the police to come in and talk to our young people, it's been very easy to have that relationship. And of course, if you get a few Christian officers coming in, they also bring the non-Christian officers, and they begin to realise that, though there might be bad PR about young Black kids, there is a Faith group of youngsters who are law-abiding, good citizens. And that helps to break down stereotypes on both sides.' (Senior worker, NTCG)

The provision of facilities and services beyond the Faith community is also a strong feature of the work at St Peter's Centre in Coventry and St Mary's Community Centre in Sheffield. The new St Peter's Centre has proved a popular venue for many groups. Its spaces can be used flexibly so that 'We have had faith groups coming from all communities: Sikh, Hindu, Muslim, Somalian groups, Afghan, Iranian and Kurdish. The list is actually endless. It's more than blossomed' (Sikh development worker).

However, just because a large range of people use the centre there is no guarantee that the benefits of bridging will be seen. It is acknowledged that:

> 'There are ways of networking but there is still a vast amount of work to be done because, what you have to remember particularly with faith groups, a lot of faith groups are very much associated with their own communities. Within their own communities they have organisations of their own.' (Sikh development worker)

The Asian People's Project at St Mary's is managed by an Asian Muslim woman. It offers language, computing and parenting classes and general advocacy, and engages with a wide range of people: young people, housewives, asylum-seekers and partners of people working in the universities and hospitals, and people of many nationalities and religions in addition to the Asian Muslim majority. The project manager gives a very positive assessment of the relation between the project and the church. She describes her work as being 'under the St Mary's banner'. In her view St Mary's is not paternalistic, seeking to do good *to* other people. She sees it, rather, as trying to give people a place from which they can build their own resources.

Here, bridge building is most evident between the professionals and other paid workers in the centre. The centre manager (also a non-stipendiary Anglican priest) identified the potential of these connections and also the long-term process of deepening relations. The St Mary's youth leader gave this review of the situation:

> 'We talk a fair bit; we're starting to work together.... It's fascinating. I've learned a lot because of [the Asian People's Project manager]. She's very aware of the Western culture as well as coming from an Asian culture. Most of us, we are ignorant really of the backgrounds of many Asian families. I learned a lot from [her] about where Asian families are coming from and how difficult it is for them to live in our society. So I'm learning a lot. I think there is a huge hurdle for Asian families to overcome, and for us to overcome, in understanding.... I just I think there's a big gap, a big gulf that needs bridging and I think we are trying to do that here.'

This mutual learning and trust between paid staff provides a basis for increasing understanding and trust between people using the community centre. Informal time between organised classes can also be important. The Asian project manager recalled an episode when Middle Eastern, Chinese and Italian women were discussing their 'home' governments' startlingly different policies on birth control – 'an example of the cultural interchange and the understanding that can build up when you've got the space to meet'. She describes one of her classes as 'the St Mary's United Nations'.

St Mary's ethnically diverse youth group has about 50 members, although they prefer the description 'volunteers' as they have active roles in running the club. Although many of them attend the same multi-ethnic comprehensive school, a significant number only know each other through the youth club. They were asked if there is any conflict between the young people along ethnic or religious lines. One said, 'No, we all get along. I don't think racism is a problem with this youth club. I reckon. Because we have different people from different backgrounds, it helps because they get to know about each other's backgrounds and religion' (teenage volunteer, St Mary's youth club). They had also developed skills and confidence germane to producing bridging social capital and democratic participation.

Social capital through engaging across boundaries

Leading on from this use of the buildings – and the visibility and exposure provided by this – is an engagement with wider forums and society which is supported by the physical presence of the buildings.

For example, GHS participates in local events and festivals and is part of the Lancashire BME Pact (a network of all the Black and minority ethnic representatives in Lancashire). The GHS building itself is well used as a venue for conferences, training and other events. Visitors come to GHS to learn about Hinduism, many on visits organised by schools. As one of the first Hindu community associations, GHS acts as a role model for Hindu organisations in other parts of the country.

The expertise and sustained presence of GHS has led to some of the leaders being co-opted onto other community initiatives locally.

'The Temple is known as a centre of activity and a strong institution in the Hindu community, and therefore

people like [the President], and [a member of the management committee] are drawn into wider networks – for example, the St Augustine's Neighbourhood Renewal Trust has co-opted [the President] onto its management group.' (Local Christian resident and activist)

Individuals associated with GHS have, over the years, also come to hold positions in other organisations that serve to bridge and link the Hindu community into wider society. The President of GHS is also the Social Inclusion Development Manager with Lancashire County Development Trust, and also well known nationally, acting as an adviser to government departments and task forces. The former community worker, still very active in GHS, is the voluntary Community and Faith Sector Liaison Officer in the Policy Unit of Lancashire County Council.

In another example, the NTCG is a founder member of the broad-based organisation, The East London Communities Organisation (TELCO – see Chapter 7). Through TELCO, the NTCG works with people from all the other Faith traditions in the locality, and other organisations, such as housing associations and community organisations, for the benefit of the area. This not only achieves improvements, but builds bridging and linking social capital between organisations and individuals that would otherwise not be natural allies. For example, the NTCG has worked with the East London Mosque.

And of course, for some very conservative Christians, going to a Mosque was a real psychological barrier. So, through our partnership working, even the way we think about the Mosque is actually different.... By the same token, we are also trying to encourage non-Christians to use our space. We've got to reciprocate.... And it means that we don't have to work in splendid isolation. (Senior worker, NTCG)

This has also demonstrated to some of the statutory bodies that they have allies in Faith groups. The police in particular have been grateful for the opportunities that the NTCG has been able to offer in relation to race relations and community cohesion.

Another key example emerges in the disturbing and controversial context of the bombings and attempted bombings in London in July 2005. These had the potential to cause severe damage to the relationships between Faith groups and communities. In west London the Muslim Cultural Heritage Centre (MCHC) played an important role in addressing this. In the days following the arrests, MCHC staff worked as 'connectors' between the local Muslim community and the police and other authorities, as well as with the wider local community. The families of those arrested were counselled and assisted, needing careful liaison with a range of statutory and voluntary agencies. MCHC staff were the connection between the national media and the local Muslim community as sensationalist and speculative reports put a great strain on local relationships.

MCHC staff and volunteers were only able to perform these functions because they were making use of existing bridging and linking social capital built up over a period of years. The Centre has followed a policy of building relationships with providers of local services, the statutory authorities and the police, while at the same time building bonds between the very different and ethnically diverse sections of the local Muslim community. MCHC is also a member of a very active and lively Forum of Faiths that is supported by the Royal Borough of Kensington and Chelsea, and that has given support at this time.

Buildings, bridges and links – critical factors

The examples above demonstrate that the buildings owned and used by Faith communities can form the basis for effective contributions to social capital, especially through providing opportunities for bridging and linking across boundaries.

Some important factors emerge as central to success. In the short term, the shape and size of the building constrains what can be done in it. But it is a characteristic of many Faith

communities in this study that their vision, even in the short term, is not limited by their present premises. In the longer-term they adapt and even rebuild.

These developments need people with vision, and the courage to change and develop that vision over time, even to demolish the old and build afresh. Of course, the fulfilment of such aspirations requires funding and a sustainable financial base. But perhaps most of all they need the motivation and drive of a few key individuals, rooted in their theological traditions, who are able to energise a large number of others. Using a combination of the bonding social capital built up within the Faith community, and the theological imperatives they interpret from their Faith, they are able also to create bridging and linking social capital.

Thus, St Mary's was rebuilt to incorporate a community centre after bomb damage in the 1940s. By the late 1980s it needed substantial reinvestment and the congregation reassessed their relationship with the neighbourhood:

> 'We then began to reposition the whole project, as we understood how you need to engage with groups in the neighbourhood, how we needed it to not be our project on behalf of the community but our project and the community's project ... their project as much as ours.' (Vicar, St Mary's)

Similarly, GHS was firmly based in the needs of a small, tightly bonded community as a key basis for confidence in their identity in a changed world. It has always relied on the dedication of a large number of volunteers willing to give their time and money. As the needs outgrew the front room of the house they met in initially, the community took out a mortgage to buy a redundant school building, and the trustees promised their own homes as security. The leadership of a number of dynamic, determined and visionary individuals was a crucial factor. They not only carried through the primary aim of the Hindu community to establish a base for itself, but also had the vision and courage to make it face outwards and make connections into wider society.

In all cases there has been a need to establish a diverse financial base, and generate income in a way that is consistent with the principles and values of the organisation, resulting in a variety of community and social enterprises.

Good local networks and relationships have been a fundamentally important resource in all the Faith communities we encountered.

> 'Relational capital has been the most significant thing of the last five years. By relational capital I mean having a network of relationships and friendships with local people that you can call upon when you need it. It might just be getting a local estate agent to write a letter in support of your project, getting the local housing association who we've allowed to use our space free of charge to write a letter of support, or saying to a local school, you can use our premises for an extra class.' (Senior worker, NTCG)

The management structure of St Peter's is of particular interest in relation to local networks. Since its inception, the congregation has been in a minority on the management committee. Only six of the members are from St Peter's Church; the rest are from four local community organisations and representatives from the streets next to the centre. 'And then, once we were away, there was a necessity to set up the management committee which again is so important to demonstrate that the church has handed over this building to an independent body to get on and run it' (Vicar, St Peter's).

This willingness to relinquish control over the running of the building is of real significance. Here we see a coming together of aspirations to inclusiveness from Faith groups and others, reinforced by the expectations that come with the use of public money. Initiatives to develop bridging social capital are reinforced by this excursion into linking social capital development, and vice versa.

There is, behind the examples chosen in this research, a driving force, a motivation that participants relate to their Faith tradition and belief. For the Christians this is related to theology, but in a practical, down-to-earth way that people can get to grips with.

> 'One aim is to try and look at how God is at work here and how we need to have our eyes and ears open and sometimes to see what is going on.... [This has] helped to shape a very incarnational, very embedded, very nuts and bolts ministry in this area.' (Vicar, St Mary's)

> 'The theology of justice must be central ... and there is a raw sense that people have got to take their own agency seriously.... It is also about offering hope.... If the theology of social responsibility means anything, our first question to you is "what are you doing about it?"' (Senior worker, NTCG)

At GHS, those involved see the work that goes on at the centre as embodying the fundamental principles of Hinduism: 'These are innate, sometimes we don't realise it or think about it academically. It is the values about integrating, about serving the community. Respect and tolerance. Making sure our Faith community is valued' (President of GHS, a volunteer).

Buildings and barriers to social capital

The bridging and linking work based on these buildings is often more fragile than at first appears. Typically it relies on a small group and is rarely seen as a priority by the majority of the Faith community. There may also be negative aspects associated with the work or internal divisions that need healing.

At GHS, the maintenance of the building and the activities takes up a great deal of energy from the volunteers. Staff members are paid now, but their role is to manage the centre and make sure it functions well and stays financially viable. For example, several schools visit, they learn about Hinduism and often have demonstrations of cultural activities. All this is done voluntarily. Representation at area-wide networks also has to be done on a voluntary basis. This puts a strain on people, many of whom also have full-time jobs and families.

Issues also surround the extent to which the potential and benefits of wider engagement are understood outside a small group of leaders. Hence, when there is competition over the use of the centre's resources, those with a strong internal agenda tend to dominate:

> 'They are mainly concerned with the day-to-day routine running of the centre. Because they lack the understanding of the importance of being connected in the wider group, because they are quite happy because the centre is successful, the centre is being used extensively, we've got income coming in, that's all they can manage.' (Volunteer, GHS)

This reliance on a few key people is also in evidence at St Mary's:

> 'There is only a handful of people really that keep the thing going ... but there are quite a lot of elderly folk that have just seen change after change after change and just want calm and come to church to receive what they can from the Church and go home again.' (Vicar, St Mary's)

A general suspicion of Faith groups is also sometimes a barrier. NTCG had experienced this in relation to perceptions of religious enthusiasm and wariness of 'religious fakes'. The NTCG also has a reputation for evangelism that can create suspicion. Working with the Muslim community has broken down some of the barriers that NTCG members had in respect of other Faith traditions, and the NTCG members found:

> '... we were able to come together without thinking, 'how can I convert these people?' We were actually saying to ourselves, 'how can we work together because we both share a religious agenda, and to some extent we have got much more in common than people of no faith?'.' (Senior worker, NTCG)

But the reach of bridging and linking also needs consideration. In the area around GHS in Preston there are some qualifications as to how deeply into the non-Hindu local population bridging and linking takes place. While members of this wider community do use the centre to access courses and activities, and individuals are invited to particular events, there may be a certain amount of '... picking up the usual suspects, people like me and the vicar' (local Christian resident and activist).

There is also some negative – sometimes ambiguous – feeling in the local community. While people seem to like the building and know that, when they go in, they have been welcomed, there is an element of jealousy about what is perceived, rightly or wrongly, to be a significant amount of funding that has gone into GHS from statutory and other related sources. 'So there is a little bit of looking down and saying, well, why can they do that for the Hindus, and not for us?' (local Christian resident and activist).

The local authority and the Regional Development Agency seem to be recognising this and are supporting other groups in the community, for example, the mosque and the Catholic-based St Augustine's project.

Summary

Bridging and linking social capital that is associated with buildings takes place in two main ways:

- through the provision of services focused on the members of the Faith tradition that also bring them into closer contact with, or increase their understanding of, the wider community; and
- by the provision of services or facilities to the wider community, which brings people together across the traditional divides of Faith and culture.

Buildings, as well as being a resource for the neighbourhood, give the Faith community a visibility and a platform for wider engagement. This platform, and the experience gained, can be used to bridge and link at a variety of levels, local, regional and national.

At the same time, there are challenges. Buildings-based Faith connections are often fragile, relying on a small group or are not often prioritised within their Faith community.

A focus on the buildings can also obscure the realities of dissent within Faith communities. And, although Faith buildings represent Faiths in very visible ways, there can still be suspicion over what goes on within them. Therefore, bridging and linking remains a relatively fragile dimension of the activity of many Faith communities, mainly because it relies on a small number of highly motivated people with the vision to see opportunities beyond the more immediate needs of bonding.

5

People in spaces

In the previous chapter we explored ways in which Faith buildings, as centres of activity and relationship, provide a focus and a physical space for social capital. In this chapter we consider how faith communities can be 'spaces' for bridging and linking in a wider sense. What is 'behind' or 'alongside' the physical places that constitutes a context for social capital? Is there something about the more amorphous spaces of people's associations with one another that supports the production of social capital? Through their various activities and interactions, we ask whether Faith communities provide distinctive opportunities for certain kinds of association between people.

In framing these questions, we also acknowledge that, in common with the rest of society, there are often issues about how many Faith groups and organisations engage and associate. Later in the chapter, therefore, we explore some less positive evidence in relation to gender and generation.

Features of association between people of Faith

The activities and relationships within many Faith communities appear to be characterised by certain features of association that support the making of social capital. There are other features that inhibit it.

These features of association may be understood as separate from the question of what social capital itself is like. Rather, they constitute the frameworks within which social capital grows, or declines. Several dimensions emerge from the episodes explored in this project. Five particular key aspects are identified:

- Faith communities 'organise' people's associations with each other.
- Faith communities can be supportive contexts for associating in new and diverse ways.
- Faith communities can inspire trust and confidence, commanding influence and power and affording opportunities for association across power differentials.
- Faith communities, through their organisational structures, bring people together in associations that are developmental and strategic.
- Faith communities can act as non-organisational networks, as in the case of Together for Peace in Leeds (see below).

Each of these features is explored and illustrated using episodes identified in this research.

Shaping people's associations with one another

Faith communities have the potential through their organisational capacities to act as 'hubs' for bringing people together in relationships, often within the framework of an overarching structure or organisation, and at international, national or regional levels. Such organisations tend to be hierarchical and to cascade down from central bodies to local levels, as in the case of the Christian Church of England. Thus many Faiths tend to be organised in ways that bring people of Faith into connection on a relatively large scale. 'Community' of this kind may be understood as encapsulating and enabling a particular kind of social capital that is very wide-reaching but that may also be rather thin. In this sense it may constitute a rather stretched form of social capital that bears little tension or pressure. Thus it provides a weak but discernible framework holding together a large and in many ways impersonal community of interest. Although it appears to rely on the bonded social capital of similar Faith communities, the depth and resilience of such bonding may in fact be rather weaker than initially perceived. Rather, its strength lies in its capacity for taking a rather thin general bonded-ness within which many people identify themselves with a 'tradition' and acting to bridge and link, often strategically.

In addition to these fairly stretched 'hubs' that 'cascade' right across a Faith community, there are also examples of smaller, more robust, forms of strategic association that exist within Faith communities to further specific aims. For example, the Churches' Regional Commission for Yorkshire and the Humber (CRCYH) was formed in 1998 when it was anticipated that the New Labour government would be open to working with Faith groups. This was recognised as an opportunity to engage with a new policy agenda and CRCYH was established as a structure for organising this. A basic initial requirement was to equip people for confident engagement: 'People need to feel confidence and some trust in engaging in partnership working' (Policy Officer, CRCYH).

Beyond this, we discovered three further consequences of the commission's formation. First, CRCYH is able to command attention because it has a good reputation and arose out of other organisations that are recognised and respected. Second, it has resources in addition to those already in existence within atomised Faith groups across the region. These resources therefore support the growing activity of networking and partnership working for which CRCYH was established. Third, CRCYH is able to take more of a 'bird's eye view' than its more local counterparts by operating across the region. Thus it is in a position to search for, identify and share episodes of activity in such a way as to make bridges and links between otherwise separate groups and organisations. This is its key contribution to social capital.

A clear example of the commission's ability to forge connections is seen in its response to growing awareness of issues of debt in the Leeds area. CRCYH hosted a 'financial exclusion breakfast' attended by local people, representatives from credit unions and financial organisations, local authority officers and councillors and Faith groups. This opened

a dialogue between the groups and sectors, which led to other initiatives for the relief and addressing of debt in the area: 'At the financial exclusion breakfast, people from different financial bodies came along and said what they felt about the issue and where they stood with this....' (Policy Officer, CRCYH). At the same time, CRCYH acknowledges that the social capital that it is able to articulate depends to some extent upon the roles, positions and attitudes of people: '... a couple of individuals in the right group at the right time' (Policy Officer, CRCYH). Yet CRCYH is able to identify the conditions that might support the growth and deployment of social capital and harness them.

Central to its role in contributing to social capital is the ability of CRCYH to mediate between the grassroots and those with decision-making power because it is trusted, known and actively networks. It develops bonds within and among Faith groups but it also bridges and links more widely across the whole region. In this way it has the distinctive characteristic of articulating Faith communities horizontally and vertically.

A second key example of a Faith organisation operating as a distinctive 'hub' for social capital is Church Action on Poverty (CAP). CAP is a national organisation that aims to link national perspectives and agendas with local experiences and activity. A key activity here is CAP's work with local groups, connecting them to a wider agenda. It is acknowledged that this depends heavily upon trust and relationships, first within groups (where trust is usually high) and then between those groups and CAP. In this example, therefore, there is a stronger relationship between bonded social capital within groups and the bridging social capital that follows between the groups and CAP. CAP then seeks to extend that bonding and bridging into linking social capital by offering engagement with others and with other agendas beyond the local. 'They trust the groups they're already part of and what we can offer is an engagement beyond their local community' (Coordinator, CAP).

A strong example here has been CAP's 'poverty hearings', which were held formally between 1993 and 1999 and continue to happen at the instigation of local groups, many of whom come to CAP for organisational support. The poverty hearings are a long-term series of local and regional events bringing together stakeholders from all the sectors and Faith groups. The hearings explore and identify key issues and solutions to poverty in local areas. This very practical approach to understanding poverty is all the more distinctive for its emphasis on including people who themselves are living in poverty. This has often resulted in very powerful presentations and testimonies making vivid issues that may otherwise have seemed merely matters of policy rather than lived experience.

One example of a concrete outcome from such a hearing was seen when a local church joined in partnership with its local authority and set up a credit union. This arose directly out of the generation of social capital between two organisational partners brought into dialogue as a result of a third.

A supportive context for relationships and associations

Another way in which Faith communities operate distinctively in terms of social capital is as contexts for new relationships and associations. Many Faith communities are able to demonstrate a strong tradition and theology of social engagement and insistence on community, sharing and love. Yet these personal dimensions of relationship also find their counterparts in the character of their association with one another.

An example here is in the work of the London Muslim Centre (LMC) in the East End of London. The LMC has a large and impressive building on a busy main road, which has been built as a result of the great determination and resourcefulness of Muslims in the area. Yet, far from being an Islamic enclave, the LMC is a highly outward-looking, metropolitan and community-orientated organisation. In this sense the building, huge and impressive though it is, is only one part of the achievement of the centre. Through its activities, the LMC has proved itself adept at associating closely with others; for example, the local authority, which made officers available throughout the planning and development of the centre to try to draw in as

wide a constituency as possible. The Jewish synagogue next door has also been a supportive partner, working with the LMC trustees in identifying needs and joint approaches to solutions. Thus the very presence of the LMC has generated social capital between Faiths and sectors as well as contributing to the further bonding of Muslims within the Faith community.

The key strength of the community, however, has been the often-informal networking of individuals within the board of trustees. Trustees have highly developed networks from the grassroots through to decision makers across the area and are able to draw on people and skills to meet needs as they arise. This is understood within the LMC as a function of cultural dispositions within the community arising out of a shared Faith and the strong relationships associated with it.

It is acknowledged too, however, that there can be over-dependence upon relationships, so that that good work falls away when individuals move on. For example, the LMC recognised that the departure of the local authority officer with whom they first worked was a significant setback resolved only as new relationships were made.

Inspiring trust and confidence

The character of associations within Faith communities can also inspire trust and confidence. This was evident in the example above of CRCYH. Yet there is a further aspect to this that is well exemplified in the work of the Church Urban Fund (CUF). This is a voluntary sector agency addressing urban disadvantage; its credibility in this field attracts the support of other funders in such a way as to draw together people in grassroots projects who might otherwise not engage with each other. This represents a form of social capital arising out of people's positive perceptions of faith groups and their distinctiveness (Dinham, 2005). This provides a platform for bridging and linking.

An example here is the New Hope mentoring programme in Birmingham. This is a partnership between Faith groups, police and the probation service, using volunteers from

Faith communities to mentor offenders returning to the community following arrest or conviction for street and drug-related crime. The focus is on young people aged between 18 and 25. The CUF provided the initial funding for this project. While this CUF finance was relatively small, the imprimatur of the organisation has lent further credibility and influence and supported the development and strengthening of strategic partnerships with other agencies. This extends in one direction to the police and probation services and, in the other, to educators and learners through the mentor recruitment strand of the project

Acting developmentally and strategically

Faith communities also show an ability to develop social capital through strategic and developmental awareness and activity. They are able to bridge and link with specific purposes in mind and add to the efforts of others to work together in pursuit of social objectives. An example of this is the Community Pride organisation in Manchester.

Established by CAP and a partnership of other churches in 1999, the aim of Community Pride is to engage with the regeneration process and explore ways in which Faith groups and the community can have an influence on decision making in Salford and Manchester. A key element of its work has been networking with community groups and Faith organisations to develop a strategic voice across the area. The organisation has played a crucial role in engaging the churches in East Manchester with the New Deal for Communities and the Commonwealth Games regeneration programmes by providing skilled personnel to facilitate the process and support church people.

'Non-organisational' networks – the case of Together for Peace, Leeds

It is not only through buildings and (formal and informal) organisations that people of Faith 'associate' in ways which support social capital. Together for Peace (T4P) is a city-wide network in Leeds. Its council of reference includes Christian and Muslim leaders, local and national politicians, representatives from

the voluntary sector and business and the Northern editor of *The Guardian* newspaper. Its formation was prompted by the terrorist attacks in New York and Washington in September 2001 and its aim is 'to stimulate the city to become peaceful on all levels' (www.networkleeds.com/index.pl?z=39). The 'centrepiece' activity of T4P is a cultural festival, reflecting the view that key channels for the exploration and expression of 'peace' are 'theatre, film, music, sport, spiritual reflection and debate'. Between festivals, T4P organises or collaborates with others in specific events, activities and campaigns.

T4P provides a 'space' quite different from those offered by most formal organisations or congregations. Although established Faith organisations have been important to the success of T4P at particular moments, collective involvement by Faith congregations is not numerically strong. The energy for T4P comes from another source: 'There will be various dynamo people that make stuff happen ... you tend to get key people getting really involved.... It relies on dynamos who are out there in their spheres to make things happen....' (T4P project worker).

Thus T4P is not strongly rooted in the collective memberships of place-based congregational communities. Rather, it is able to draw on more dispersed interest communities. Many bridges and links are made through the organisation of the festivals and cooperation in major initiatives such as the Hiroshima/Nagasaki exhibition.

Issues of association – the cases of gender and generation

The preceding sections have identified some important positive consequences for social capital that stem from association between people in Faith communities. However, we have also encountered some problems and barriers. These are explored here with particular reference to the experience of women and young people. We recognise that there are also likely to be issues with regard to ethnicity, sexuality and disability but these have not been a focus of our interviews and did not emerge in the encounters we had.

Although they are not addressed here they are important matters that should be addressed in future research.

Gender and social capital

Many of our interviewees observed that women do most of the work in community activity. Nevertheless they become less visible the further one moves from grassroots activity, and the higher one goes up the ladder of decision making. Faith groups are sometimes criticised for according a poor status to women, and for barring them from the tiers of decision making. While Faith groups and institutions are open to this criticism, it is important to remember that this is an issue with which wider society is also struggling.

In this research we were looking for examples where Faith-based groups were involved in linking and bridging. The gender balance of the people this led us to interview was roughly 30% female and 70% male, although this is slightly distorted as a quarter of the females were associated with a youth group and were interviewed together. We did not set out to achieve a gender balance, nor specifically to investigate the role of gender in social capital, but took what opportunities we could to find examples of people engaged in bridging and linking social capital.

Women are clearly engaged in generating bonding social capital in Faith organisations and were present in every venue and project visited. However, when it comes to engaging in bridging and linking, it is mainly the men who are involved, or at least it is the men who speak about this on behalf of the organisation. There are exceptions to this. In one organisation where all staff members were women, the interviewer remarked that, in many community organisations, the work was done by women but the men make the decisions. The senior worker being interviewed responded by saying, 'It's not like that here. We [the women] decide what to do and then we get on and do it'.

Some Faith groups have separate, parallel organisations for women and men. This is sometimes perceived by outsiders as limiting women's power, but for the women involved it

can be experienced as enabling. One of the interviewees said that she had managed to develop the women's side of a mental health drop-in much more effectively than the men had. However, it was felt that this was associated with a 'power dynamic'. The same interviewee said that, when she had been overall project leader for the mental health project and had developed the women's side, the men's group had not made the same progress. Since she left, and a man was overall project leader, the men now feel they have a link to the leadership and their side is developing well: 'I think the women accept the man [in authority]. Men have difficulty with a woman' (female member of staff). Many organisations provide specific initiatives for women. One had organised an event called 'Women's Voices', an opportunity for refugee women to tell their stories (although the interviewees talking about this were men).

In another place, and from a different Faith, one respondent who had been associated with a Faith-based community organisation for many years, and had taken a leading role in developing its bridging and linking work, spoke with sadness about her decision to resign from the management committee because of the attitude of some of the men in positions of power. She said she had received support from a few, and that had sustained her for a while, but the overwhelming experience was of being blocked when she tried to have an influence at strategic and policy levels.

> 'Breaking the glass [ceiling] I think is always going to be difficult, no matter where you are. I can definitely say that gender is a big issue.... They don't want women in this position because they see that as diminishing their role as men.' (Female volunteer and former management committee member)

Nevertheless, women also frequently find ways of getting the decisions they want by indirect means: 'Well, let's say we have to do things in certain ways because there are certain things that are acceptable, and certain things that aren't, but we can get round them' (female member of staff). So, in Faith-based organisations, as in the outside world, women use indirect methods to exert influence and get the results they need. For some, like one of our respondents, the pressure eventually becomes too great and they leave the organisation.

One Faith organisation that has been addressing the exclusion of women from the decision-making structures is a Black-led church in East London. The constitution allows women to be active in all aspects, including being ministers, but not to be members of the decision-making pastoral council. This leads to the anomaly of a woman minister not being part of the pastoral council that governs her church. This church has decided, in contravention of the constitution, that women should play a full part on the pastoral council. 'So, in our Church, it's a sore issue internationally, but it is one that we have resolved here just as a matter of practicalities, biblical theology, and just pure justice' (male staff member).

Similarly, in a New Deal for Communities (NDC) area in London, Muslim women have been working together to change the cultural restrictions that prevented them from participating in the community processes. The timing and venues for the meetings meant that they could not attend as they were expected to be in the home. One dynamic and determined woman decided to do something to get the voices of these women heard. She started a group that met at a time and place that the Muslim community found acceptable. Their views were then fed into the NDC process. Gradually, the women developed the confidence to start to challenge some of the traditional cultural constraints. Others in the community, chiefly the men, came to appreciate the contribution of the women, and to realise that it was not a threat. The women now participate more freely and have begun to set up their own support networks.

Generation and social capital

Here we consider the often differing perspectives of different generations and, in particular, the opportunities of young people in Faith communities to be enriched by social capital and to contribute to its formation.

Several middle-aged leaders reflected on the attitudes of their parents' generation, informed by the experience of migration to the UK some

50 years ago: 'I listen to many of the elder generation from the Caribbean and one of their most profound statements was, "I don't want my children to go through the same suffering we did"' (African Caribbean church leader). The same people see their own youngsters exhibiting rather different attitudes: 'Today in our community the younger generations will accept individuals for who they are, irrespective of colour, creed, religious belief or cultural understanding. That fear within our elder generations is almost gone' (African Caribbean church leader).

On various occasions leaders of all the main religions in the UK have indicated their concern at the loss of Faith among young people or, perhaps more accurately, an unwillingness on the part of young people to follow in their parents' Faith tradition. In relation to Hinduism, one woman commented:

'I think in the way that we were brought up, on a very practical level, going to the temple, doing the worship, we didn't have the understanding. We were told stories about Ram and so on. We weren't relating that to how that impacts on our lives. We know that we shouldn't be consuming alcohol and drugs, but we don't know why. We don't know whether the religion is telling us not to do it, or whether it's customary or tradition, or because that's how it was in India or wherever.'

We secured a group interview with leaders of a youth project drawn from different Faiths. One of the group recalled a workshop on the theme of 'community cohesion' and expressed scepticism because, 'It's natural to be in your own community', and 'Community cohesion is more than race; it means something to me provided there is equality'. Initially, this discussion about cohesion paid little or no heed to the religious background of the young people, but when this theme was introduced it was as though in these settings 'permission' to talk about Faith was needed. Their aspirations were clear; they were trying to bridge between different groups. In doing so, they do not distinguish between ethnicity, culture and religion. They use these terms relatively interchangeably.

'In the forum we are not racist or anything like that. We never have any barriers. You do get it outside, obviously, in the community but not in the forum. We are trying to change that and that is our message. We want to get away from all that so we are trying to get representation from everybody and link different communities together which don't normally get together.' (Sikh, female)

When the conversation turned to an exchange about life at home and in college, however, other factors surfaced with a bearing on Faith and social capital. One of the young people remarked upon the extent of suspicion between groups at college:

'In some cultures, I think it's a bit beyond help in a way. The college that I'm at, I hate it there because there is so much racism to the Sikhs and the Muslims. If you walk into the room you have a corner of Sikhs and a corner of Muslims and if you speak to the Sikhs then you don't speak to the Muslims on that day. You can feel the tension.' (Christian, male)

The young people explain these circumstances in terms of ethnicity, culture and religion, a mix that has established attitudes and behaviours over the years. When asked to comment on whether their respective Faith traditions encourage bridging to others, their viewpoints are mixed:

'Well, they say it does, but I don't believe that it does. A temple, anybody can come in, anyone external, whatever religion you are, you can come in. But to be honest I don't think they do. Sikh people do not like Muslim people at all and they don't like a Sikh girl talking to a Muslim guy, at all.' (Sikh)

'With younger people we have been brought up in this area so it is just normal. It is just the way that things go really.' (Christian)

'I have loads of White male mates and Muslim mates and stuff like that. I think all the other Asians in the school; they were a bit wary of going round speaking to people from different backgrounds. I wasn't. I used to go up to them and speak to them and just hang around with them and I used to get dirty looks from them.' (Hindu)

These young people are clear that their experience in the youth project has opened their eyes to people of other backgrounds. Their perspectives on the contributions and barriers to social capital in relation to Faith communities are important. The implications of their views and experiences prompt the following three observations:

First, encouraging attitudes are exhibited by many of these young people in discussing their relationships to people from other backgrounds. They show a clear willingness to seek bridges. Second, some Faith leaders anticipate that when current young people are in positions of greater power and responsibility within their Faith networks, there will be change. They predict a greater understanding of difference and a greater willingness to engage with others, formally and informally, to meet wider community needs.

Finally, these young people are critical of the insularity of the Faith groups they have experienced. They might well value the bonding provided by these groups and the sense of support and security this gives but, at the same time, they challenge the traditions and attitudes of the older generations. They do not want them to give up what is core to their Faith, but their comments do contain a questioning of some attitudes and traditions. The young people want their concerns to be heard.

Summary

In this chapter we have examined several ways in which people of Faith and their communities associate within and between each other and with the wider world and, in the process, develop or inhibit social capital. Some general, mainly positive, factors have emerged from the contexts and episodes that we have explored. Other, sometimes more negative, issues emerged from our focus on issues of gender and generation. Overall, the following findings can be identified. First, Faith communities are capable of *articulating* interaction between people that is purposeful, even where that purpose is debated and its methods unclear. People of Faith want to work together in pursuit of social goals, even though they may not know what they should be or how they should be achieved. Second, Faith communities are capable of contributing to the *organising* of the bridging and linking necessary for shared purpose and action.

6

Participation in local governance

Our central research question asks: 'How far can Faith organisations and their members contribute to social capital that not only bonds people together in bounded communities, but also enables them to cross boundaries and participate in wider, looser networks and forums in a democratic society?'. In this chapter our interest is in what encourages or discourages the development of linking social capital when Faith communities participate in local governance so that they might exert greater influence and access resources. What happens in their relationships with local authorities through Local Strategic Partnerships (LSPs) or participation in neighbourhood management initiatives?

Evidence comes from three sources. First, research on Faith communities' involvement with urban regeneration provides a useful introductory perspective. Interviews that are concerned with the more formal partnership arrangements in cities and conurbations provide a second perspective. Finally, four examples of initiative at the level of the neighbourhood demonstrate something of the complexity of the Faith contribution to linking social capital.

Faith and urban regeneration

Some aspects of this issue were addressed in earlier work involving some members of the present research group (Farnell et al, 2003). Explicit discussion of the notion of social capital was absent from that study but interviews with professionals and people of Faith working in regeneration allow conclusions to be drawn. In particular, the development of linking social capital was inhibited by:

- a lack of 'religious literacy' among regeneration professionals;
- a perception among religious groups that they are discriminated against in the allocation of funding;
- difficulties in engaging minorities, women and young people;
- some incompatibility between secular and faith definitions of appropriate gender roles and equal opportunities; and
- competition and sometimes conflict within, as well as between, faith groups (Farnell et al, 2003, p 39).

This present research has allowed a revisiting of some interview transcripts from the previous work, with these matters in mind. These interviews illustrate good and bad experiences of Faith groups engaging with urban regeneration policy, practice and people.

Faith leaders and regeneration professionals were encouraged to tell their stories of regeneration. Personal stories and organisational histories were requested to provide a context for their comments and opinions. This section draws out significant factors from these stories, grouped in relation to interviewees' judgements about whether their experiences of linking were good or bad.

Positive experiences

From the perspectives of the regeneration professionals, interacting with Faith groups was more likely to be productive if a number of conditions were fulfilled. First, they valued those initiatives that originated in local communities. If the ideas are conceived and nurtured by local people who have a stake in that neighbourhood then they own them: a factor that provides greater confidence for linking with professional agencies. This is especially so when the Faith group is recognised and accepted as part of the wider community. If opinion demands that 'we must do something', the move from a sense of despair to hope is quickly identified as 'good experience'. 'But the secret of the success of the Furnival isn't that somebody up there somewhere decided, 'Let's do this!' Actually there were four elderly members of a Methodist chapel who refused to give up and believed that something could happen there' (Christian interviewee).

Second, professionals indicate that they like to see people working together. Cooperation within the neighbourhood is valued, especially when there is a crossing of boundaries created by background, ethnicity and self-interest. Bridging social capital is the result. External support from statutory agencies (linking) adds significantly to the sense of partnership:

> '"Faith in the Future" is now beginning to build credibility. The Housing Corporation put funding in to enable this offshoot to actively involve the Faiths in regeneration but starting from a Muslim base. It's significant because it's a Muslim-led inter Faith initiative, led by young people.' (National regeneration professional and Faith leader)

A 'model' process is seen when such partnership working is informed by a resolve to be patient, because it takes time to get to know people well and to build up the relationships that will lead to effective action. The significance of visionary and entrepreneurial leadership completes the picture. These are characteristics of social capital.

Third, professionals point to the importance of a thorough and well-defined assessment of the local situation, identifying both needs and demands. This forms the basis for deciding on action and engaging positively with other groups and agencies. The most successful projects are those with the capacity to respond multi-dimensionally, with a range of interrelated activities, because there are usually many needs and demands. It seems that bridging and linking social capital are mutually reinforcing.

This type of experience described is not, of course, unique to Faith involvement. Neither are the bad experiences reported below.

Negative experiences

Faith leaders identified four sources of discouragement in their engagement with governance. First, there is evidence that some Faith groups feel excluded from regeneration activity. This is usually expressed in the sentiment that 'nobody consulted us!'. Sometimes invitations to participate come too late, when decisions have already been taken. Repeated consultation but a lack of action produces the following response: 'I think I'm a cynic. It's very frustrating. Some people are saying, we're fed up with being consulted! If you want to know, you go and find out your own ways' (Muslim interviewee). The quality of communication between statutory agencies and Faith communities is an important issue.

Second, many Faith leaders tell stories about the difficulties experienced by religious organisations in obtaining public funding. This is especially so when the group has as one of its objectives 'the promotion of religion': 'The attitudes have sadly still remained with a lot of the funders that if an idea is coming from a Faith community, straight away they say, "Is it the promotion of religion?"' (Muslim interviewee).

Those with direct experience of funding processes and regimes regard the bureaucracy as excessive in volume and complexity, the timescales as impossible and the grant rules as inflexible.

Regeneration professionals and Faith leaders make similar points concerning, first, the bureaucracy put in place in the attempt to achieve fairness and accountability and, second, the capacity of both statutory agencies and faith groups to engage effectively in regeneration activity.

The language and practice of statutory regeneration is often a problem for community representatives. Their concerns relate not only to bureaucratic procedures but also to the use of jargon, the operating style and the external pressure to meet deadlines. All these matters can lead to the decision to 'pull out'.

Third, Faith leaders recognise that they often lack expertise, skills and capacity to engage in public regeneration processes. A need for improvements in leadership, management and financial control is articulated. But they are also aware that the regeneration agencies themselves also lack capacity, particularly in employing people with an understanding of Faith communities.

Fourth, Faith leaders tend to focus on the quality of their relationships with regeneration professionals and politicians. Broken promises lead to decisions to withdraw and disappointment follows if funding bids fail. 'Linking' social capital can be hard to create and maintain in such situations.

Faith leaders readily acknowledge that there is potential for competition between groups, which can bring accusations of malpractice in their wake: 'Conflict between communities, where one community feels that they've been badly done by because another estate got more of the allocation, is bad' (Sikh interviewee).

Funding criteria may be interpreted differently in relation to the bids of different Faith groups. In these circumstances, it becomes clear that there is often a close relationship between the two types of social capital. Undermining one will have a negative effect on the other.

These negative experiences provide a window on the complexities of linking social capital. All participants consider that there is little capacity on either side to make steady progress on engagement. Professionals also comment that the pressures of work lead to an obsession with crisis management rather than the challenge of constructing agreed strategies and meeting with people face to face: 'Well, I've learnt in regeneration that it's not what you say, not what you write, it's what you do. You need to be visible and that's how they learn to trust you' [local regeneration professional]. The development of trusting relationships is central to notions of social capital. The importance of constructive personal contact cannot be over-emphasised.

Among some professionals there is scepticism concerning the motives of Faith groups, which reveals itself in the search for hidden agendas. For others there is a view that Faith groups sometimes have unrealistic expectations, have undertaken insufficient investigation of their situation, and lack clarity about their basic aims. If regeneration professionals bring these suspicions to the table, social capital will be difficult to build. If the suspicions are accurate it will be impossible to build it.

City-wide partnerships

Over the last few years there have been initiatives to create 'Faith forums' in regions such as the West Midlands and Yorkshire and Humberside. In addition, the creation of LSPs in all local authority areas in England, together with 'community empowerment networks' in the more disadvantaged areas, has spawned attempts to create partnerships between Faith communities themselves and also with these new instruments of official governance. While these Faith groupings might be formed for various reasons, one commentator observed:

'What worries me about faith networks … associated with LSPs is that they can become obsessed with purely getting together to create linkage into the power structure.

I am not convinced that these networks are actually generating on-the-ground activity.' (Diocesan partnership officer)

Although practice varies from place to place, there are questions about whether it is either desirable or, indeed, worthwhile to create structures that provide for one or two 'Faith representatives' on a 100-person-strong regional assembly or a 40-person strong LSP board. Creating a Faith forum on the assumption that this will then provide a mechanism for authenticating representation and guaranteeing accountability is doubtful. Such approaches may have validity in the short to medium term, but it is unlikely that they can provide adequate longer-term structures. Nevertheless, it needs to be acknowledged that networks, forums or partnerships of these types have enabled certain Faith community leaders to meet and engage, thus enhancing levels of bridging social capital.

However, other interviewees comment on the limited nature of such partnership work, particularly in its seeming inability to challenge thinking and action:

> 'Yes, they engaged with the city un-politically. They go to the city council, which is behaving like a great patron in order to build up the vision of a great city. The notion that there could be serious political arguments about the nature and purpose of the city; that, I don't think, is there at all. There is the general assumption that we are all nice people together.' (Christian, male interviewee)

This raises questions for both Faith groups and agents of government about the purpose of engagement with the structures and processes of local governance and whether a degree of clarity can be obtained before engagement.

Neighbourhood initiatives

Perhaps activity in the neighbourhood has more potential to reveal what encourages or discourages the formation of linking social capital. Certainly, our respondents confirm that grassroots involvement in governance necessitates a degree of bridging if linking is to be achieved. Four episodes in four different locations provide insight into the development of social capital in a context of Faith.

Making a public commitment

The first case involves an initiative by an organisation formed in a northern city to help community groups, especially Faith groups, to be involved in regeneration processes. No pre-existing Faith network was able to respond to opportunities for involvement brought by the introduction of a New Deal for Communities (NDC) programme. A community development worker tells the story, as follows:

> 'Anyway, we had a workshop day. We looked at the NDC process and the churches were actually fairly critical of the whole process. Now it might have been the way we constructed the event, because we were coming at it from a critical perspective. What that served to do was nothing constructive, at all! It actually marginalised the churches from the regeneration process.
>
> So the churches had to go on the back foot and look at how they were going to engage with the regeneration process in a constructive way. So they set about developing this 'Regeneration Pledge' and we got about 200 to 250 people together for a big ceremony, where all the church leaders signed this pledge, which effectively committed them to being involved in the regeneration for the benefit of the community.
>
> In terms of bridging social capital this was quite interesting. We've got the Black African Pentecostal churches linked up with high Anglican and Roman Catholic and then you've got all sorts of Baptist, United Reformed and Methodist churches. It's a real mix.'

But,

> 'It's been a bit of a reactive process to be honest and in that sense I don't think it's been that good. My personal opinion is that the churches as a group haven't done anything particularly constructive within the regeneration process. They've had this dialogue and individuals have been involved.
>
> But, as a group, the churches have never really had a particular direct involvement with the process and that's a disappointment to me.' (Community development worker)

This episode contains two, mixed, sets of messages. On the one hand, a critical initial stance contributed to a marginalisation of the churches from the NDC process. On the other hand, with support, there was a re-thinking of their approach and a clear public pronouncement about commitment to the neighbourhood. There appears to have been little joint activity from the churches but plenty of participation on the part of individual congregations and people. The interviewee provided an explanation that many would recognise from other circumstances and cities:

> 'Let's take the inner city churches that I'm familiar with. I would say the majority of them don't bridge and link because that takes a level of energy that they don't feel they've got. Bonding is easy because you pitch up on a Sunday morning, you're all there. Bridging requires going out into your community and making links with other people.' (Community development worker)

Making a partnership of interests

A second case involved a multicultural neighbourhood in the West Midlands, one that had seen City Challenge expenditure in the 1990s. In 2001 a partnership of local community interests was established, including Christian, Muslim and Sikh organisations. Two years later, as part of experiments with 'neighbourhood management', a process was set in motion to develop an action plan, using the Planning for Real approach.

For this research, a group interview was undertaken with seven leaders from Muslim, Sikh and three Christian communities with significant African Caribbean memberships – Church of God of Prophecy, Anglican and Methodist. Considerable understanding and trust had been built up between these leaders over a number of years with all but two active in the neighbourhood for at least 10 years. Their conclusions about the involvement of their Faith communities in local governance revealed a real sense of achievement, but also a disappointment that the quality of relationships shared by them was not experienced by more local people:

> 'Faith-based establishments like mosques, churches and stuff play fantastically huge roles within the community. Our community is not large in its demographics and area but what happens, I would say, well over 50% of the activities in some shape or form has a strong link, or more than that, have a strong link to faith. It's all interlinked, entwined.' (Muslim)

However, despite the support that people of Faith give to their neighbourhood and their willingness to participate in one-off events such as the Planning for Real consultation, the 'Faiths walk' around the area and the street celebrations for the Queen's Jubilee, the continuing, week-by-week, involvement in the activities of local governance is limited to just a few people.

> 'But, the other thing that I think one has got to say, is that in the Faith communities, as elsewhere, it is a very tiny proportion of the people who are actually pushing these community things and it is actually still true that the Faith community as a whole doesn't easily get outside its own walls.' (Christian)

Involvement is sometimes in the face of situations that, by definition, discourage the process of building linking social capital. In this neighbourhood-management exercise the feelings are expressed as follows:

> 'I will have to be careful how I say this, but in terms of processes, they will light a bit of a fire and then as soon as the fire starts to grow, they will pour water over it. So what they have done is that they have started the passions burning, but in reality they don't make it sustainable. Once the momentum is lost to re-ignite that community's passion and stuff, it doesn't work.' (Muslim)

These seven Faith leaders reveal in their thinking and behaviour various resources and understandings that provide them with the means to cope with such frustration:

> 'I think this is a multi-cultural and multi-religious society, especially in this area, and they are living very peacefully. They respect each other's faith. If they don't understand each other's religion and what their religion says, they still respect each other.' (Sikh)

'I think there is strength in Faith communities. They produce a social cohesion which produces a network of mutuality and they can sustain that mutuality. We've passed the initial stage so we can give space for the other. So we are learning something about diversity and difference and how diversity and difference can be held together in some unity.' (Christian)

'There are certain parameters within Faith which enable a coping with divergence and catastrophe. There have always been catastrophes around here and, therefore, the nature of faith gives us an ingredient to forbear one another, a bit! It gets a bit frustrating sometimes. You drive each other up the wall....' (Christian)

'So there are principles within my faith that drive me. I am not after the money. The work that I am doing has reward hereafter. As a believer in God I am doing this; it is not for my own benefit. I am doing it for the benefit of the community and what I believe in.' (Muslim)

Linking to public agencies

The third case is taken from a neighbourhood where a Jewish voluntary organisation took the initiative to apply for funding for a Sure Start project to provide for younger children. This attempt to link into public agencies encouraged the development of bridging social capital at the same time:

'We decided to make a case for having Sure Start. So we got together a shadow partnership which comprised many agencies including the local Muslim community, who have similar issues to our own and so we involved them. We involved some church organisation and other groups, both statutory and community. And it's been a success, we were chosen as a Sure Start area.' (Jewish voluntary sector manager)

The reasons given for working with people of other Faiths and no Faith are interesting. As in the previous example, the motivation is essentially pragmatic; they face the same issues.

'It wasn't from any sort of idealistic ... it was just purely pragmatic for children in our area. And we find that it is actually the most successful way of doing something rather than from sort of a political point of view. A pragmatic approach is very good. Everybody stands to gain; everybody is interested.' (Jewish voluntary sector manager)

Working together on common concerns has other consequences which reinforce the development of bridging social capital:

'Well, I think they achieved mutual respect. So they achieve what they set out to achieve, an alleviation of deprivation and better opportunities for children and families; also a widening of horizons because you learn from each other.' (Jewish voluntary sector manager)

Taking the initiative

The fourth and final case is also small-scale. Ten years ago two adjacent parish churches in a medium-sized Midlands town decided to establish a 'church plant', an offshoot of the main churches, on a council estate. The church meets for worship in the small community building at the centre of the estate, next to the playing field. Most people attending the church live within half a mile of the community centre, including two households immediately opposite.

For several months one of the church leaders had been trying to arrange a meeting with the police officer responsible for the estate to discuss the use of the play area and the needs of local children and teenagers. A meeting was arranged at the community centre one mid-week evening. The story continues:

'I was supposed to be chairing a meeting of, at the most, six people. Sixty-five turned up ... and they were cross! Somehow, knowledge of the meeting had spread through the estate and people came to what they thought was a public meeting. Two local councillors got wind of it and came as well. For an hour and half there was argument and counter-argument; regular shouting and muffled apologies.

At the end, promises were made about policing on the estate and a decision made to meet again in three months.

Three months on, there were not just district councillors, but county councillors, too, plus a prospective parliamentary candidate, the police superintendent, sergeant and officer, the community support officer, the local authority head of housing and community services and a couple of consultants!

By the end of this meeting commitments had been reviewed and further promises made about policing. But, in addition, overwhelming votes were taken to establish a new residents' association, two neighbourhood watch schemes in different parts of the estate and a family mediation service within a particular close. Subsequently, the town-wide credit union has opened a collection point in the community centre.

The church people are thoroughly involved in all these initiatives, as participants like everyone else.'
(Church leader)

In this case, a rather simple initiative, with little expectation of results, produced extensive outputs, albeit ones which have yet to prove sustainable in the longer term. Some see it as chance happening; others talk of serendipity; others see it as answers to prayer. Whatever the explanation, change has happened because this Faith community took an initiative without knowing what the consequences would be and without wishing to keep ownership of what followed. The willingness to initiate and to relinquish control has some resonance with other research evidence. Such an episode may not be common, but neither is it unique. The willingness to 'let go' or to 'go with' the

unexpected seems a significant element in building bridging and linking capital.

Summary

This chapter has explored some experiences of Faith communities in the development of linking social capital. It has reviewed evidence regarding those factors that encourage and obstruct the engagement of people of Faith with processes of local governance, for the benefit of their neighbourhoods and communities. Some of these matters are common to all organisations in local communities, whether Faith-based or not. We can identify four particular barriers to sustainable links:

• There can be failure to deliver on promises after raising hopes about what might be achieved and difficulties in working through what are seen as bureaucratic processes.
• Lack of capacity and understanding by Faith groups and government agencies leads to poor communication and suspicion, countering the trust that is central to the growth of social capital.
• There are divergent expectations between Faith groups and public agencies. Agencies look for willing compliance from external bodies while Faith groups have their own, sometimes challenging, agendas.
• There is often a limited number of people in Faith groups in disadvantaged areas with the energy and commitment to be involved in local governance.

On the other hand, there are four qualities, the presence of which encourages the development of linking social capital:

• Practical action that grows out of the local situation and in which other diverse groups can share, stimulates the development of linking social capital. Government agencies have a role to play in welcoming such initiatives.
• Government agencies should recognise the existing presence, activity and achievement of individuals, single groups and partnerships. This will stimulate further desire to build social capital.

- In the face of frustration and setbacks, religious Faith has the potential to contribute courage, hope and self-sacrifice, rooted in an acceptance of mutuality and a respect for difference.
- The willingness of some Faith communities to 'step out in Faith', taking risks in responding to need in their communities, yet without demanding continuing ownership and control of the initiative, should be acknowledged.

7

Participation in the 'public domain'

In Chapter 6 we assessed the extent to which Faith organisations and their members contribute bridging and linking social capital through their participation in governance networks and partnerships framed strongly by central and local government. We have seen that this involvement has underlined the significant positive contribution made by Faith groups, their limitations, and the barriers that they confront. Participation in this mode of governance can also shape, restrict and even erode the social capital that Faith communities contribute. In this section, however, we examine Faith involvement in a less regulated 'public domain'. This has been defined as 'the domain of citizenship, equity and service whose integrity is essential to democratic governance and social well-being', a domain with a distinctive culture (Marquand, 2004, p 1).

Of course, the idea of a public 'domain' is an ideal. There is no totally discrete sphere of citizen association untrammelled by state and consumerism. Indeed, many commentators have identified an erosion of the public sphere. Their response, however, has been to press for enlarged space for a much more local politics and the development of strong 'intermediate associations' (see for example Hirst, 1994; Marquand, 2004; Chapman, 2005). We explore here the capacity of Faith groups and their members to work with others to address this challenge through participation in pluralist and deliberative democratic forums. Our focus here, therefore, is on the engagement of Faith groups in open-ended and negotiated 'associational' politics rather than as providers of government-approved 'social glue'.

Citizenship of this kind has been described as an 'unnatural practice' (Oldfield, 1990 – quoted in Hill, 1994, p 14). The ability to participate as a citizen in a political community demands qualities and skills that require *development*. Within this overall field, therefore, this section focuses on the actual and potential capacity of Faith organisations to motivate and equip people for engagement in the public domain, to contribute to the bridges and links, and the ability to work with 'difference' essential to associational politics.

This chapter assesses these issues in two related contexts: first, the 'congregational development' programme in the diocese of Sheffield; and second, 'community organising' (CO) alliances in which Faith groups are prominent members. Of course, these do not begin to exhaust the full range of initiatives. Moreover, CO has generally stood apart from other strands of British community development and has been the subject of criticism as well as affirmation (Farnell et al, 1994; Henderson and Salmon, 1995; Furbey et al, 1997). Nevertheless, it is explored here as a significant example of an attempt to make connections, one that illustrates the present potential and limitations of 'Faith' social capital in the public domain.

Congregational development in the diocese of Sheffield

We must not equate congregational and institutional life with the 'bonding' of similar people. Many congregations are internally highly diverse and the challenge of living, and worshipping, together can be intense. Bridges are important *within* as well as beyond.

People's development within local associations often sustains their capacity to operate on a wider stage. Faith communities have long been places where people have developed personal confidence, skills, qualities and awareness that have equipped them to operate beyond their 'base'. There can be significant development from involvement in worship itself. Religious beliefs often prompt the acceptance of civic obligations.

However, the practice of active congregational participation – dealing with disagreement without rowing, 'withdrawing', leaving or splitting – may require capacities that still need to be explicitly *developed*. Indeed, the processes of deliberative congregational 'citizenship' can be particularly perplexing for members of Faith communities where authority is located not just (or even mainly) in the popular will but also, and variously, in prophet, priest, tradition and scripture. Jonathan[3] at St James' Church identified a particular issue:

> 'I think something that holds churches back is an atmosphere of 'niceness' and politeness – the feeling that, because we are all Christians, we all have to get on in a happy kind of way. Whereas, sometimes, the situation demands a kind of seriousness that's not really compatible with what is being 'polite'.'

It might be added that, without this 'seriousness', things can stop being 'nice' very abruptly.

The 'parish development consultations' offered to Anglican churches in the diocese of Sheffield draw on a growing Anglo-American 'congregational studies' literature (see, for example, Cameron et al, 2005). Subjecting the familiarity of one's worship community to this perspective can be unsettling, making relative a world that has been experienced as being as natural as the weather. Or it can permit positive sentiments, deep frustrations or 'dull aches' to be explored in a helpfully detached

way as a basis for productive and enriching action.

The participatory training workshops in the Sheffield diocese are facilitated by the diocesan development officer, who is an ordained priest with past and present experience of work with diverse congregations. A member of the research group observed at two consultation workshops involving members of St James' Church. Both workshops involved around 20 participants and the positive response to the content and approach was reflected in the high proportion of church members who returned on the second week.

The facilitator explained that a basic aim of the sessions was 'to help you 'learn to learn', not as individuals but as a body, a congregation'. This aim was then addressed by activities that encouraged participants to discover their own unique parish 'wisdom'; that is, 'the way we do things here'. This 'wisdom' was explored by activities that involved:

- assembling and reflecting on a 'parish story', using the differing experiences of longstanding and newer members;
- exploring the consequences of congregation size on organisation, authority structures and the scope of mission;
- identifying the present main purposes of the church and those that participants would like to prioritise in the *future*; and
- assessing the nature and the extent of a shared church 'outlook' among participants.

At each stage, therefore, participants were enabled to make the implicit more explicit. For example, St James' is experiencing a slow growth in membership and needs to address the issues of moving from a medium-sized to a large congregation. In such a situation, the role and skills required of the vicar may need to change as part of a wider process of organisational change. Or, in identifying the different preferred future purposes of the church, possibilities of both opportunity and conflict come into clearer focus. In addressing these issues, the identification of either a shared outlook or divergent outlooks again has potential value in recognising a shared dynamic or sources of division as a first step to working with differences. Thus, the key intended outcome of the sessions was to

---

3 Individuals and churches are given pseudonyms in this chapter.

prompt a shared ongoing revision of the 'parish wisdom' that incorporates and works with this new awareness. The facilitator expressed the inherent challenge in these terms:

> 'We can offend other people by doing things that, to us, seem entirely rational. The irritation is the result of our mutuality. No one way is right. It is the result of our coming together.... The maturity of a congregation is seen in the recognition of this mutuality and responding to it positively.'

But he also noted that there can often be a 'culture of evasion', not least in the Church of England, that needs to be countered by the ability to be assertive and 'straightforward'.

Community organising and citizen development

Developmental work with religious congregations or organisations, extending to 'institutional' development with secular groups, is also a key element in the activity of community organising. Here, however, this training is one aspect of a wider campaign to achieve the development of citizens. The developmental work of CO is focused more explicitly on equipping people to campaign and to form stronger bridges with other groups, not just among a common, albeit diverse, membership. This section assesses these developmental activities of CO and their contribution to bridging and linking social capital. First, we provide a brief orienting sketch of this community development tradition.

Sketching community organising

CO stems from the work of Saul Alinsky (a secular Jew) in Chicago in the 1940s. His essential approach to community development and campaigning remains significant in the US. An important source of funding for CO in Britain has been the Church of England's Church Urban Fund. There is an element of self-funding through the payment of dues by

member organisations. CO organisations have not sought state funding.

At the time of writing, The East London Communities Organisation (TELCO) Citizens in East London was the largest and most consolidated CO with 37 member organisations (www.telcocitizens.org.uk). Birmingham Citizens was in the initial stages of development, while IMPACT in Sheffield, with 26 member organisations, was in a state of suspension following the cessation of Lottery funding (www.impactsheffield.org.uk). South London Citizens was inaugurated at the end of 2004 with 19 member institutions (www.southlondoncitizens.org.uk) and developments in West London are underway. The London initiatives form an affiliated group, London Citizens. The aim is to build civic organisations that bring together an alliance of diverse secular and Faith 'member communities' around 'the shared humanitarian values of justice, dignity and self-respect'. In practice, however, Christian congregations and other Faith organisations form a majority.

CO seeks to tap grassroots concerns through intensive 'one-to-one' encounters to establish people's key concerns. The aim is to give people a democratic voice as citizens. This informs the identification of 'actions' whereby, through careful research, strong internal organisation and accountability and dramatising large-scale 'assemblies', an explicit attempt is made to apply power to secure change. These actions can range from limited initiatives, such as the relocation of a pelican crossing, to TELCO's Living Wage campaign, which has involved a challenge to major corporate employers, and IMPACT's Sheffield-wide financial inclusion initiative, building on earlier neighbourhood projects in Sheffield.

The process of equipping people for democratic participation is an explicit objective, as signalled by the extract from IMPACT's aims below:

> Our aims are to bring together a wide and diverse set of local congregations, institutions and associations into a civic organisation that will encourage members to act together on issues and concerns they share. This process of co-operation, compromise and learning

together about power and politics is challenging stereotypes, sectarianism and discrimination. We aim to build relationships of trust and mutual respect between an increasingly diverse group of community, workplace and religious leaders by working together around a shared vision and by agreeing specific, achievable steps towards making this vision a reality.

The process of solving problems and the active and regular participation of the organised people of Sheffield in the decisions that affect their lives, is as important as the vision itself. This will strengthen and enhance the democratic process and help the local member organisations to develop and train their leaders. (www.impactsheffield.org.uk)

What are people's experiences of participation in CO? Do people experience personal and collective development as citizens? Are bridges built and links made?

Leadership training

In November 2004 a member of the research group observed and participated at a two-day non-residential community leadership training workshop organised by London Citizens. There were 39 participants, 14 from Christian churches, one from a Christian school, six Muslims, one Baha'i, two from educational institutions, three from Filipino organisations and six from other organisations, including one from a trade union.

The workshop was highly participatory and elicited positive responses. Many participants spoke of the importance of working together. There was also evidence that the event generated some new understandings and increased trust. One female participant was initially very negative about the workshop, explaining that she had been sent on it by her manager. At the end of the workshop she was much more positive about London Citizens and also said she had changed her view about Faith organisations and their role in the community. This sense of bridge building and the achievement of new understanding was also reflected in one of the last workshop

sessions, when people were asked about the aims of CO and why their organisation might (or might not) join. Their answers, paraphrased, included the following:

- It celebrates diversity and uses it.
- It unites communities.
- We can actively participate and build partnerships.
- By building relationships with others, small organisations can become more effective.

These responses reflect both a pragmatic recognition of the advantages of 'bridging' and a more value-centred motivation for working with others.

Community organising and congregational development – the case of IMPACT

The experiences of individuals in IMPACT development workshops and in working across boundaries with other, 'different', membership communities were explored through group interviews with members of three congregations in Sheffield. The extent of success in building various bridges was further explored through interviews with the IMPACT organiser, one of the organisation's directors and a leading member who is also a Muslim community leader. The IMPACT organiser provided this description of the organisation's congregational and institutional development work:

'It is basically five sessions, an hour and a half for five weeks, looking at what's going on within their congregation or their institution. What does that institution mean to the outside world? And where do they fit into it [their organisation] as an individual? And it starts with a very intensive piece of work for me, doing as many one-to-ones as I can, going out and having conversations with people to get a picture of where they think their institution is and how healthy it is, but more about them as well. You know, who they are, why they do what they are doing … all those kind of things. And then what it ends with is with them having a short plan about going forward. And then it's up to them.'

The sessions have a strong component of participation and provoke questions and awareness regarding the internal relations of the membership and its wider place in city and society. Interviewees were positive in their assessment. Richard offered this assessment of the benefits of the sessions at St Margaret's:

'I thought it was very good because it was a way of trying to explore and break down the barriers within your own community, based on the premise that communities are about knowing people. And that is something that we didn't take that seriously and ought to.'

Ruth identified a tangible benefit in the reflection and subsequent action on organisational efficiency at her church. Of the sessions, she said:

'They were good. I enjoyed them. It enabled us to think. We came up with lots of ideas and some of them were put into practice, but not others. It brought home that we do lots of talking and not a lot of doing, and then we moan that things aren't being done as they should be done and we never get around to changing them. And I think that holds not just for the Parochial Church Council-type things, the structural things, but other things on in our lives I think really.... So it was personal development, I think, as well as congregational.'

For Matthew, the value of the meetings and their group exercises was in the way they permitted expression of concerns and differences: 'I think it enables us to bring dissatisfaction to the surface and we did resolve quite a few misunderstandings at the time.... That was good'.

Overall, the workshops provided a context to enable participants to step back from their 'congregation-taken-for granted' and to reassess its inner structures and relations and its role in the public domain.

Beyond the workshops – positive experiences

What have been the practical experiences of IMPACT members beyond these workshops in practical 'actions' and campaigns? The reactions of interviewees were again broadly favourable, although there are some less positive experiences reported, some of which reflect the wider limitations of CO reviewed later in this chapter.

One of the study congregations was an Anglican church in one of the most affluent districts of Sheffield, with a history of close association with the city's business establishment, far from 'bottom-up' campaigning. Matthew, an older member of the church, recalled early projects – prior to the formation of IMPACT – that involved tentative crossings of Sheffield's strong geographical class divide:

'It was a very interesting project. We all went to other parts of the city, and I remember when somebody from [St James'], born and bred in Sheffield, went up to the Park Hill flats and said, 'Do you know, in forty-odd years I have never been here'. It was things like that that I remember very vividly.... We visited various families; just two of us would go and be linked with a family....'

Another Anglican church affiliated to IMPACT is in a former mining area. IMPACT has been strongly supported by the vicar and, until its recent suspension, there was an active core group of about six church members, with other members participating at key actions and events. Richard reflected on his experiences through IMPACT:

'For me, it was the learning about people who were in dire poverty in a city where you wouldn't expect it to be. It's not that I go round with my eyes shut, but you move in the circles that you move in, and you don't tend to come across it.'

Catherine is a member of a large Roman Catholic church in Sheffield. She spoke positively about IMPACT as a vehicle for building connections across religious denominations, Faith traditions, and between her church and secular community groups: 'I like the idea of IMPACT because it's such a varied group – it's not just, sort of, church groups, it's other Faiths as well and I think that's got to be a good thing if you're bringing people together'.

Sheffield has small Jewish, Hindu and Sikh populations. IMPACT's ability to build bridges between Faith traditions, therefore, was explored in relation to connections between Christians and Muslims, more sizeable groups. The evidence here is mixed. Some of our interviewees affirmed the value of Muslim–Christian connections and understandings made through IMPACT. Graham at St James' made this assessment: 'I gained a huge amount of understanding of the Muslim culture and how there are similarities in so many ways between us and Muslims'. For his part, the Muslim leader described the invitation to participate in IMPACT as 'the best gift I have received' because:

'They welcomed me and also worked very closely with me. They've arranged for me to go to many churches where I have gone and given lectures.... So it has given me a platform to give the positive image of Islam, not the caricature portrayed by the media, and also has helped me to get to know the other side, the Christian faith.'

Nevertheless, this inter Faith bridge as developed within IMPACT is quite narrow and reliant on particular personal relations of trust. This is one of several limitations that may be characteristic of both IMPACT in particular and CO more generally. It is to these that we now turn.

Limitations and obstacles

We noted above that CO is only one approach to community development and campaigning. Moreover, it is controversial and often criticised. Its American origins and cultural style, if not amended for a British context, can be inappropriate and encounter resistance.

First, our research in Sheffield and London suggests that only a minority of people within member organisations are actively and regularly engaged, although others may be mobilised at key points for actions and large assemblies. In each of the Sheffield congregations visited, there were between five and 10 people who had been regularly working with IMPACT. Of course, this is a familiar situation in many other organisations. The activists, with the support (or perhaps the toleration) of others, can often play a productive part in CO and prompt their 'home' organisation to become more outward looking. Nevertheless, the lack of a larger base is a source of frustration for those involved. As Frank at St Margaret's recalled: 'I was very disappointed towards the end, at the actual number of people from all these communities who turned up for some of the meetings, because that had really dropped....'.

This causes a second difficulty. Despite its formal aim to 'build from below' through one-to-ones and the development of its members, CO has been charged with authoritarianism and a concentration of power in the hands of leaders, often the paid professional organisers, or member organisation leaders, including clergy. Richard at St Margaret's voiced this concern:

'One of the things that I found through IMPACT – and it's something I was trying to wrestle with – is the fact that the paid staff who are supposed to be employed by IMPACT, by the very nature of the fact that they are in there all the time and hour-on-hour learning about it ... you come to have a meeting on financial exclusion or financial inclusion and to a certain extent you're rubber-stamping what they've decided, purely because they've got the knowledge.'

Without a strong membership base, the accountability of CO leaders may be weakened. Much depends here on the quality of leadership, including that of member communities. Support for CO is often more broad-based and sustainable where the leadership is democratic and empowering of members. In all three of the Sheffield congregations, past or present vicars facilitated and motivated members' engagement. At St Margaret's, Richard made this observation:

'[Something] which I think is very important in our parish is the way Steve [the Vicar] enables people'. In an earlier separate interview Steve stated his priority in this way: 'When I leave, you know, there won't be a gap – that, actually people will have the church that they want, the church that they feel is important'.

Third, rather than maximising its bridges, we have noted the tendency for CO organisations to stand apart from other strands of community development, limiting the various 'capital' resources that stem from wider networks and risking the dangers of a closed and potentially authoritarian culture. IMPACT seceded from the main CO network in Britain precisely to avoid this pitfall. Even here, however, in an otherwise very positive report, an independent evaluation noted that IMPACT, at least in its earlier years, 'appeared not to recognise or appreciate the value of the work other organisations had undertaken to good effect over many years [and] has appeared to be an arrogant in-comer, taking for itself credit more properly shared with others' (Pinder, 2004, p 8).

However, the report finds evidence of subsequent 'healing' of relations with other organisations and urges further bridge building and mending. It also recognises the costs of networking and the exhaustion that can stem from 'partnership' and the need for a balance between cooperation and confrontation for a campaigning organisation.

This latter tension is especially sharp in the context of the building of 'linking' social capital. Some in government and business have experienced the pressure applied by CO organisations as unjustified and lacking in respect, a complaint which is commonly made against CO. On the other hand, in its development of its impressive financial inclusion initiative, IMPACT worked effectively and collaboratively with the local authority, banks and the Treasury. Indeed, it is the perception of some that so many of the organisation's limited resources have been poured into what is effectively a partnership that it has been unable to sustain its core activities of bottom-up one-to-ones, institutional development, action planning or securing its financial stability. On the other hand, the establishment of a high-quality city-wide credit union and access to low-cost loans and financial advice is a significant contribution to social justice and social inclusion. It has been a vehicle for participation, learning and development in the public domain and a means of developing bridging and linking social capital.

Fourth, as in several other contexts reviewed in this report, Christian communities are very prominent in CO organisations that claim to be broadly based. The relative lack of secular member communities imposes an important limitation on bridge-building capacity. Moreover, the connections with other Faiths in CO organisations can be fragile, as illustrated by the example of the Muslim–Christian link within IMPACT in Sheffield. The context, certainly since 9/11, is clearly demanding. The organiser of IMPACT, a White woman, described the diversity of Muslim nationalities and mosques in Sheffield, their varied outlooks, the difficulties of engagement and the need for patience: 'They rightly suspect White Christian organisations, which they would see IMPACT as being.... It takes a long time to build relationships and you have a lot to prove.... For an organiser to build relationships with those organisations that don't trust us, it needs a long time'. Meanwhile, she suggested, 'there are key stakeholders within all the ethnic minorities' and she identified the importance of the existing personalised link with Muslims in Sheffield: 'He is a gatekeeper and without his respect and help then it would be very difficult to go anywhere. But once you've got it...'.

Finally, the recruitment of member communities has proved not only a crucial task but also a difficult one for CO. The size and financial stability of CO organisations in England and Wales has never matched that achieved in the US. Of course, there are wider social, political and cultural factors that operate here. However, as alliances of 'value-based' organisations, CO may appeal particularly to groups with an explicit statement of values and beliefs. These may or may not be founded in religious beliefs, but the consistent preponderance of religious member organisations, particularly Christian churches, may discourage some secular groups.

Moreover, even within the 'religious' category, there is wide diversity in the values, beliefs, practices and experiences associated with different religious understandings and there are predictable participants and absentees. We saw in Chapter 2 that there are doctrines and traditions in all major world Faiths that both prompt and inhibit social engagement and working with others. Nevertheless, groups affiliated to CO are likely to be those with relatively clear social theologies or understandings rather than those characterised more by individualism and pietism. The religious or humanist roots that motivate involvement may also produce organisational volatility as well as energy. As expressed by one former community organiser, drawing from these 'deeper wells' can be 'a hostage to fortune as the slightest failing can bring a charge of hypocrisy or can lead to the exodus of member groups who demand exacting moral and ethical standards' (Waters, 2005). More prosaically, the small size and intense internal life of many member organisations, and the pressing needs of their 'own people', are obvious barriers to involvement.

Restricted membership is a far-reaching constraint. CO in the UK has been marked by limited and precarious funding and several organisations have failed to survive. Yet limited funds and activists can serve to compromise and slow still further work that, as we have seen, requires patient long-term development.

building linking social capital as organisations engage with their own regional and national hierarchies, with governance and with business.

There is a need for a wider audit of similar initiatives than has been possible in this research. Both the initiatives explored here have strengths, but they do not exhaust the possibilities in this field and they have clear limitations. Key issues for their survival and future development are the level, source and timescale of funding of this essentially long-term work. Financial independence from the state in this particular field seems crucial but, as the history of CO in Britain has shown, funding from other sources is elusive. The potential benefits of recognising and supporting this process of development within organisations can be considerable as this local practice of democracy is reflected in the strengthening of social capital in wider contexts. It offers an alternative to an engineered or imposed consensus as Faith communities participate with others in a more active and autonomous association.

Summary

Institutional and congregational development through the congregational training programme in the Diocese of Sheffield and through CO are two contexts in which members of Faith organisations and others can develop their capacity to operate in democratic and deliberative forums. Although small scale they represent counters to the common undemocratic cultural undertow in many Faith (and non-Faith) organisations. They are potential instruments for the development of bridging capital both *within* groups and organisations and also for bridging and mutual understanding and support between individuals, groups and organisations *across* social divisions. These skills and qualities of democratic practice can also build capacity in

8 Conclusions and implications

Our guiding research question has been:

- *How far can Faith organisations and their members contribute to social capital that not only bonds people together, but also enables them to cross boundaries and build bridges and links with others in civil society?*

Our summary answer is:

- Faith communities contribute substantial and distinctive bridging and linking social capital through their co-presence in urban areas, their connecting frameworks, the use of their buildings, the spaces that their associational networks open up, their engagement in governance, and their work across boundaries with others in the public domain.

- But more could be done if they did not face various obstacles: the misunderstanding and suspicion of others, financial barriers, inappropriate buildings, state managerialism and regulation, and various issues of capacity.

- Also, changes and developments need to occur within Faith communities themselves. Although practice varies considerably, it is often the case that: bridging and linking is undertaken by quite a small minority; the potential skills and contributions of members may remain unrecognised, constrained and suppressed and issues of power marginalised; and the particular qualities required for wider associational deliberation and political participation often are not a subject of explicit reflection and development.

This summary contains a range of conclusions that point to implications for particular audiences. First, Faith communities, organisations, groups and networks themselves face challenges to their existing ways of working, internally but also in relation to each other, to civil society and to government. Developing a capacity to engage in open and accountable ways is one example. However, there are also challenges here for many public and voluntary sector agencies committed to the achievement of stronger and better communities, operating nationally, regionally and locally. Thus:

- Local authorities, primary care trusts, police authorities and other such agencies have to develop a much more sophisticated understanding of Faith communities with much closer relationships if latent social capital is to be used effectively. Recognition of the significant contribution of Faith organisations and their members in neighbourhood and civil renewal remains uneven. There are messages here for New Deal for Communities initiatives and for those allocating Neighbourhood Renewal Funds.

- Local Strategic Partnerships and Regional Assemblies have often taken significant strides towards the involvement of Faith communities. But our research evidence suggests that there is still much to learn about genuine engagement.

- Local authorities are now required to prepare Community Cohesion Strategies, bringing them into closer engagement with Faith communities. This research offers guidance on the qualities that should characterise these developing relationships.

The overall research conclusions are now developed further under five headline paragraphs. Implications for policy and action are identified and advanced to inform a wider

Appendix B: Interview schedule for project/activity leaders and managers

This tape-recorded interview is obviously 'on the record' and material drawn from it may find its way into final reports and publications. We shall not normally name individuals in those reports but organisations and agencies may be identifiable. Until the point of publication the information you supply will be kept confidential to our research team members. We shall provide you with the interview transcript as soon as possible for your comments and corrections. At that point you may ask us to ensure that any sensitive comments that you have made are treated as non-attributable background.

The research is funded by the Joseph Rowntree Foundation and is a follow-up to the publication last year of 'Faith in Urban Regeneration?', which involved some of the present research team.

We are interested in the concept idea of social capital and faith communities, taking a broad definition of social capital as being the connections among individuals – social networks and the norms of reciprocity and trustworthiness that arise from them.

In other words, the resources that stem from **relationships**.

A number of types of social capital have been identified:

Bonding: within communities of substantially similar people, close-knit groups.

Bridging: connections between people who have less in common, but may have overlapping interests e.g. between different groups in a community (different faith groups could be an example of this).

Linking: links between people or organisations beyond peer boundaries, cutting across status, and similarity, and enabling people to exert influence and reach resources outside their normal circles.

Our research is focused on the last two of these, the bridging and linking forms.

We want to explore the extent to which faith organisations can or do contribute to the bridging and the linking social capital necessary for well-connected communities.

We are also looking at the extent to which faith organisations may themselves constitute obstacles to the development of bridging and linking social capital.

Biography and organisational details

First, I should like to ask you about your own experience and the role of your organisation in this field.

1. What is your current post and role?
2. What is the role of your organisation in the field of faith organisations' involvement in the wider community?

3. Can you give me a brief initial sketch of the main experience that you have had of our area of interest? – we can develop the detail later in the interview.

Examples of bridging and linking

4. Given the definitions of social capital, can you give me any examples of where and how faith organisations are (or have been) engaged in creating social capital of the bridging and linking types?
5. Does this activity lead to networks and connections between organisations and people who would otherwise remain unknown to each other?
6. Can you give me examples?
7. Does this activity foster new understandings of others?
8. Can you give me examples?
9. How far has the activity produced solidarity and practical support? *(Probe: what is your evidence for believing this?)*
10. Has it helped to diffuse, or lessen conflict and mistrust; or to stop this developing? *(Probe: what is your evidence for believing this?)*
11. What else do you think these activities achieve?

Individual participation?

12. Why do you think individual members of faith organisations participate in this linking and bridging activity? *(Probe: does it connect to their religious beliefs?)*
13. What do you think has been the effect on participants? *(Probe: have they changed? Has their view of their faith changed as a result of participating in this type of activity?)*

Obstacles

14. What obstacles have been encountered?
15. How is the close-knit community bonding often associated with faith related to people's ability to connect to wider community and civil life?
16. Have there been any inequalities apparent?

Is there anything else that you think I should know that you haven't had a chance to say?

Thank you for agreeing to take part in this research.

Appendix C: Interview/group interview schedule for community/organisation members and users

This tape-recorded interview is obviously 'on the record', and things that you say may find their way into our writings. We won't usually name individual people but it may be possible for a reader to identify you or your organisation. Before publication, the information you give us will be kept confidential to our research team members. When we've written up the interview we'll send you a copy for your comments and corrections. At that point you may ask us to make sure that any sensitive comments that you have made cannot be traced to you.

Our research is about the experience of people and their organisations as they live and work together in the community. The people that we are talking to may be members of religious organisations or they may be members of other community groups.

We are interested in your activities and experiences within your group or organisation. We are also particularly interested in how much you find yourself/yourselves sharing space and activities with other groups and what your experiences are of these bridges with other people and their organisations. And we are also keen to know about any links that you have with official organisations beyond the local community like the local council or business organisations.

Our research is being funded by the Joseph Rowntree Foundation.

About you and your group/organisation

First, I should like to ask you a bit about yourself and your organisation/community group.

1. Do you live nearby, or do you travel in to activities and meetings?
2. How long have you been coming to this place and/or been part of this community/ organisation/group and taken part in its activities and/or used its services?
3. Why do you come here? (*Prompt: for company, for worship, for the lunch, to work with others to achieve community objective, as an expression of faith or moral commitment, etc*)
4. Can you tell me about what goes on here? (*Prompt: can you tell me about a typical meeting or activity?*)
5. Could you tell me about what you yourself do here? (*Prompt: use services, take part in activities, have roles or responsibilities?*)
6. What do you like about being a member of this group/organisation or using its services? What do you gain from taking part? (*Prompt: does participation give you confidence, purpose, a sense of acceptance, etc?*)
7. Are there any things that you would like to be different here? Are there any things that you don't like or find frustrating? Are there things that the group/organisation needs but finds hard to get?

Experiences of 'bridging'

8. Can you tell me about the range of people that you meet through this group/ organisation?

9. Do you meet people here with different backgrounds to your own? *(Prompt: if 'yes', could you say a bit more about this?)*

10. Have you shared any activities together?

11. Have you managed to get to know these people and develop trust and understanding of each other?

12. Have you been able to help or support each other at all?

13. Do you see each other outside of meetings/ activities, in your neighbourhood? *(Prompt: if 'yes', please can you describe. If 'no', why is this?)*

14. Is it a good thing to meet people outside your normal circle? *(Prompt: if 'yes', ask 'why is this?')*

15. Does meeting with people (or sharing the building with people) outside your normal circle bring any difficulties or concerns? *(Prompt: 'why do you say that?')*

Experiences of 'linking'

(Note: 'members' and 'users' may not be best placed to perceive 'vertical' links with local and national government, businesses, national religious or secular organisations etc. So these questions and discussion here may be limited or even inappropriate. But in other cases [eg in a context of community organising], people may have been drawn into encounters with organisations 'further up' and gained confidence and empowerment in the process. So the approach here has to be on a case-by-case basis.)

16. Through your involvement with this group/ organisation, have you become more aware of its links with the wider world the local council or with funding organisations or with national or international organisations? *(Prompt: the local council and its councillors and officers, local government officers, official regeneration programmes, official 'partnerships', national or international religious organisations or missions, business organisations)*

17. Have you had any direct experience of these links? For example, have you been involved in any meetings or activities that have involved people from 'outside' who have resources?

18. If so, what has been your experience of this involvement? What have you learned from it? Has it been a positive or a negative experience for you?

19. What caused you to get involved?

Thank you very much for your help with our research.